# ONE LAST THING

# ONE LAST THING

*How to Live With the End in Mind*

Wendy Mitchell

with Anna Wharton

BLOOMSBURY PUBLISHING

LONDON · OXFORD · NEW YORK · NEW DELHI · SYDNEY

BLOOMSBURY PUBLISHING
Bloomsbury Publishing Plc
50 Bedford Square, London, WC1B 3DP, UK
29 Earlsfort Terrace, Dublin 2, Ireland

BLOOMSBURY, BLOOMSBURY PUBLISHING and the Diana logo are
trademarks of Bloomsbury Publishing Plc

First published in Great Britain 2023

A catalogue record for this book is available from the British Library

ISBN: HB: 978-1-5266-5875-3; TPB: 978-1-5266-5876-0;
EBOOK: 978-1-5266-5871-5; EPDF: 978-1-5266-5872-2

2 4 6 8 10 9 7 5 3 1

Typeset by Newgen KnowledgeWorks Pvt. Ltd., Chennai, India
Printed and bound in Great Britain by CPI Group (UK) Ltd, Croydon CR0 4YY

To find out more about our authors and books visit www.bloomsbury.com
and sign up for our newsletters

*Who else could my final book be dedicated to, than my daughters Sarah and Gemma – simply thank you for being you*

We have two lives, and the second begins when we
realise we only have one.

Confucius

# CONTENTS

# FOREWORD

Death. It's a strange place to start a book. It is, at first glance, the end. There is nothing more final, nothing more inevitable. Death is the great equaliser, however much we try to avoid it. It depends, of course, on your religious persuasion as to whether you believe there is life after this one, or just a black abyss. That is not what concerns me as I write: what awaits us after we have died we shall have to discover when we get there. Better to focus on another journey, the one towards the inevitable – a journey that I now find myself on.

Those who have read my previous two books, *Somebody I Used to Know* and *What I Wish People Knew About Dementia*, will know that on 31 July 2014 I was diagnosed with young-onset vascular dementia and Alzheimer's disease. At the time, I had a busy job working as a rota manager within the NHS, I had raised two girls as a single mother, I was a keen runner, and the diagnosis stopped me in my tracks.

I sank into a deep depression, all too common after diagnosis of a life-limiting illness. And completely understandable. We all know we're going to die, but it is, for the most part, a luxury that we can afford to push far back into the horizon of our minds. Instead, we busy ourselves with life, with waiting for the next holiday, counting off the days that separate us from weekends, or we wish the now away and convince ourselves we will live more happily once we shift that stubborn half a stone, or stick to our promise of good food and exercise. There is always something lying in the future that will make us appreciate life more totally. Perhaps it's what we call hope, a wonderful part of the human condition – but hope relies on time. And we don't all have that.

A diagnosis of a progressive or terminal illness takes that hope away, or at least it dulls its bright beam so that in the interim it feels impossible to see through the dark clouds that descend.

I still remember those dark clouds, that hopelessness. I have said many times before that dementia is a bummer of a diagnosis and you could apply that to any progressive or terminal illness; there is no getting away from it. But I think my own diagnosis was made harder by the attitude of medical staff. I assumed it was the end because they didn't tell me any differently.

There are some who, having received such a diagnosis, stay in the dark clouds, struggle to find their way back into the light. Perhaps they think there is no point. After all, we live in a society that seems to value more the able body or able mind. But during my own journey living with dementia, I realised that my particular progressive illness had a beginning and a middle, as well as an end, and when there was so much life to be lived in between, why was my mind racing towards those closing chapters? Perhaps it was a case of wanting some control over the cards that life had dealt me, a way of convincing fate I had got there first, that its cruel surprise had failed.

I felt it so strongly that I wrote in both of my books that there is hope after a terminal or progressive illness, and I still believe that to be true. I also wrote how these same diagnoses can sharpen the mind with regards to living in the present, how they make many of us who are living with them – living, not dying – more mindful of living for the day, in some ways leaving us more alive than we were the day before our diagnoses. That is our incredible human instinct for survival, our ability to see the light through the dark clouds.

Living with dementia, nine years on, the clouds descend more frequently now. What keeps me going during those foggy days is hope – hope that tomorrow will be a better day. But, more often, one day becomes two, becomes three, four, five, and the fog hangs around, making my thoughts all sticky with glue. But the hope still cuts through – tomorrow might just be better. I comfort myself that while that thought is still able to burn through, I have not gone over the edge. I am still me, not quite the Wendy I used to know, but recognisable.

But I am aware that there is an edge now, even if I cannot see it as it comes closer. I am aware that more days after I finish writing will be spent in the fog – until the day when I don't find my way back out again. And so I would like to turn my attention to the end. That is why I have started this book with death.

If I have been able to adapt to life with a progressive illness, I would like to think that I will be able to adapt to life with the end in mind. Here, at the beginning of this book, I wonder what that looks like to others and what it might look like to me, and I am going to invite a whole host of people to come and discuss that with me – and you. I will ask the questions that we all might have: what will the end look like? Will there be pain? Is there anything I can do now that will make me more comfortable? Is there anything I can do to hasten that ending if I feel I may suffer? I will be accompanied, as ever, by my partner in writing Anna Wharton, who has co-authored both of my previous books. On the days when the fog has descended and mixed up my thoughts, she will ask the questions for me.

I invite you to read this book as if you are joining in the conversations between Anna and me and the people we have asked to share their experiences. Some of the stories and the answers will be sad, others will make you laugh, but I would like you to read as if you have pulled up a chair, cup of tea in hand, and you are sitting at the table alongside us. Pause at the end of them if you like, and write some notes about what you think.

Please do not fear: you will not find anything frightening within the pages that follow. I am not trying to tell you how death must be done, or how it should feel for you. I just want to gently remind you that one day it will come, and the more prepared you are, the more conversations you are able to have with medical professionals and with those you love, the more empowered you will feel to live in the now – and you don't need a progressive or terminal illness to do that. I will share with you how I feel about death, and some of what I reveal might surprise you. Be sure not to let it make you feel sad; know that I am making my own choices as far as I can, as one day you will make yours. I would like to be a light that guides the way.

See this book as a gift, a focus on the present by glancing – just a peek – into the future. And with that, we better get on with the business of living, and to do that, we need to talk about death.

Wendy Mitchell

Autumn 2022

# CONVERSATIONS ON DEATH

'I mean, what on earth do you use coconut milk for?'

I was sitting in my living room opposite my friend David. He was recently bereaved, well, we both were – his wife, Sylvia, was my best friend. We were both suffering a loss, and yet, his question still amused me. I know Sylvia would have giggled too.

'She never got the chance to tell me,' he said.

And a quiet descended on us.

I wrote about losing Sylvia in my second book. I wrote about what it feels like to grieve as someone with dementia, how this disease in my brain had whittled me down to two emotions – happy and sad – and yet, although it is a cruel, cruel disease, dementia offers gifts sometimes too. In my case, after losing my closest and dearest friend to ovarian cancer, dementia numbed the grief somehow. It meant that I could feel overwhelming sadness that I would never see Sylvia again one moment, and then the next be laughing about something entirely unrelated. It must have been a strange thing to witness, and that day, it was coconut milk.

Sylvia had so many plans once she knew she was dying. She wanted to teach David to cook but she never got the chance, and so it is only now that he is reaching into the dark recesses of the kitchen cupboards and finding tins of exotic produce like coconut milk and wondering what the hell he is meant to do with them.

Sylvia and I had been friends since 1995. I had met her when she was my boss, the one person who had given me a chance to prove myself working on a hospital reception, this single mum of two daughters who had, for years, been making a living as a cleaner. It wasn't long before Sylvia and I were inseparable. We saw each other through many life traumas: the death of parents; the death of marriages; and much joy too, weddings and births. David knew that if there was one person who knew what Sylvia used coconut milk for, it would be me.

'It was her secret ingredient in curries,' I told him.

It was me, three decades before, who had taught Sylvia how to make a curry, but it was her own idea to go off in search of ingredients that would improve my recipe – typical Sylvia. She'd read somewhere that coconut milk was what she needed, and so that became her thing. Friendships are like that, aren't they? A constant give and take, a swapping of ideas, an exchange of advice that can often last a lifetime, and even longer in this case. When I received my dementia diagnosis, Sylvia was there for me, helping me research, keen to know more about the trials I was taking part in. She told me I was her inspiration when she received her own cancer diagnosis; she approached her own illness in the same way, determinedly, researching trials and treatments.

'I'm strong like you. I can face this,' she said.

Now it was my turn to support her as she had supported me. But I wished desperately that we could switch places or, more accurately, that I could take that cancer from her body and put it into my own, yet not burden her with dementia. It seemed to me that Sylvia still had so much life left to live, a new husband who she adored, all those adventures they needed to have. Whereas I had already been diagnosed with a life-limiting illness. I know I said it to her, several times, that I would gladly take her place if I could. It didn't seem fair that here I was, manufacturing my future from what I could still do each day, with no real plans or long-term thoughts – I could have easily factored death into my own waiting game. Whereas Sylvia had real plans, desires to fulfil, real reasons to live. It was me who could have made more use of death and allowed Sylvia to continue living. But even as I said those things to her, I knew how meaningless, how hollow, they must have sounded, because life just doesn't work like that.

Perhaps because I had been diagnosed with dementia before Sylvia's cancer diagnosis, we assumed that I would be the one to depart our friendship first, but that was not to be the case. Her texts to me were always positive, even when the news wasn't good. Sylvia didn't worry about the future; perhaps she had taken the same lesson I had from dementia – to live in the present – and so, like me, she would often text saying: *I'm a little under the weather today, hopefully all will be better tomorrow.*

We didn't know Sylvia was running out of tomorrows.

Christmas 2020 passed in that blur of wrapping paper and carols, and I didn't receive my usual text from Sylvia on the 25th. I messaged her the next day, sensing something was wrong in a way only a best friend can.

*Now it's Boxing Day, I will have to admit I'm in hospital,* she texted back.

She knew how much I enjoyed Christmas and had been determined not to spoil the day for me with bad news. When I chastised her for it, she came straight back saying I would have done the same if the roles were reversed, and that I couldn't argue with. Her determination was still there, but I could sense sometimes that hope was fading. Having had a visit from her consultant after Christmas, her text read: *Their toolbox seems to only have bits and bobs now, whereas in the beginning it was full...*

The texts became less frequent, shorter. I knew she was spending precious time with her family. I kept in touch with David more and he told me how Sylvia was doing. The penultimate text I received from Sylvia in January 2021 read: *Still one day at a time until I fall asleep...*

The last text, four weeks later, began: *Farewell, my dear friend...*

Sylvia died a week later.

Sylvia knew that the only way to grant herself – and by extension those she loved – a peaceful death was to meet it with acceptance, to get everything in order, say all that needed to be said.

Sylvia was her usual calm and organised self in those final months and weeks. She sat with her family and planned her funeral, talked with David about how things might feel after she'd gone. When she went into hospital, she said it was good practice for him to get used to her not being there at home with him. She always thought of others, right up until the end, and I know – *knew* – Sylvia well enough to know that she would believe thinking of yourself is pointless, as that road is already mapped out; it will be the people left behind who have to carry on.

Sylvia's death reminded me that even in our darkest moments there are still glimmers of light, there are still ways to control the ungovernable march of death – a march that we shall all face one day. There are joys to choose more of, there are words of love that need to be shared; never before has it been necessary to call a single day, a single hour, a single moment, a *present* – it is, after all, a gift. I am comforted that my friend made the most of every single day she had left — even if she didn't get round to explaining to David what she used coconut milk for.

But then, that's what friends are for.

I don't fear death; I don't fear anything any more. I have written before how, pre-dementia, I was afraid of everything: the dark; animals; of dying when my girls were still children. But when I faced the diagnosis of dementia in 2014, all those other fears melted away. What more was there to be afraid of when I had faced my worst fear — anyone's worst fear — that of losing my own mind, the very essence of what made me me?

I have focused in previous books on all the living we have left to do, even after a diagnosis of dementia. But I have to be honest: death seems something of a gift now, a release from this disease that came to claim me before I was ready.

What I am left with, though, is fear for my daughters, and the question of how to make my death more comfortable for those who will be left behind — just like Sylvia did. Perhaps this is the anchor that ties us to any stormy sea: the people we love. Without love we could bob along quite happily, let the waves take us anywhere of their choosing. It is love of others that keeps us tied to life. No one can argue that love is anything but a precious gift to each and every one of us, even if it is also the source of our greatest sadness – after all, we wouldn't feel the hollow, crying emptiness of grief if we had not enjoyed the pleasure of loving.

In 1963, a survey was carried out by psychiatrist Professor John Hinton to examine the attitude of those dying in Britain. It found that often patients were not told explicitly that they were dying; often they were not even told they had cancer, as it was a word that promoted so much fear. Professor Hinton believed that those who were not able to come to terms with their death suffered more physically. Of the thirty-eight dying people he interviewed in hospital during the course of his research, none of them had been told by medical staff that they were dying, although for some, death had been alluded to by their priest. In his essay *Dying* he wrote how acceptance of death promoted 'peace of mind'. He also wrote how:

Many dying show their kindness and become, perhaps, more noble in spirit than they have ever been. They do all they can do to spare the feelings of those they are going to leave behind to bear their loss ... they demonstrate their affection in both apparent and in subtle ways. Given sufficient spiritual and bodily help, it is probable that most of those moving steadily towards death would experience the peace of surrendering to their fate before they drift into permanent unconsciousness.[1]

If it has to happen, drifting into permanent unconsciousness doesn't sound like a bad way to go. And it does have to happen. There may have been all kinds of medical, surgical and pharmaceutical breakthroughs over the last few decades, but death is still a certainty for all of us. Professor Hinton stated that his research revealed three questions that dying patients wanted reassurance about: How long would it take them to die? Would there be severe physical suffering? And would the suffering be relieved?

Hinton's research was carried out in 1963, and yet aren't these still the questions that we would all like answers to? And aren't they still the questions so many of us are afraid or unable to ask? How can you begin to understand what your questions are if you can't even talk about dying? As I've said many times about being diagnosed with dementia and fathoming life after a diagnosis of a progressive illness, you don't know what you don't know. But if we can find a way to pose the questions, we can perhaps alleviate the suffering, and by alleviating the psychological suffering, potentially also alleviate physical pain.

[1] John Hinton, *Dying*, Penguin Books, London, 1967.

Sylvia had been the epitome of plan for tomorrow and live for today; she was also the first close friend that I had seen die. That overwhelming loss came as a shock to me; we didn't live near each other, and yet all those miles between us and I still knew she was there for me. Goodness knows how David must have felt, padding around in their empty home alone, or how her daughters coped without dear old Mum to call on for advice. As a friend, I comforted myself with my belief that robins appear as the souls of those who've died. In my second book, I mentioned a dream I had just days after Sylvia had died, of a robin that came and sat in my hand, looking right into my eyes, and then promptly pooing into the creases of my palm. Yes, without doubt, that was my Sylvia. It made me laugh at least, and when people we love leave us, the legacy that they leave behind are these shared jokes that you know the other would find funny, or the memories of each other that you had held dear. They never fade, even if the skin and bones of them do.

I am not afraid of the black nothingness that awaits me, but what I am scared of is going over the edge, changing beyond all recognition into somebody I really don't know. I want to be able to talk about these feelings, just like Sylvia wanted to talk about getting ready to die. Perhaps my need is more pressing. There are some days when I wake up and the fog has blurred the path ahead of me to the point that I don't know where the edge is – am

I about to topple over, or is there more path than I think, more footsteps to take? This is how it feels for many of us living with a progressive illness; it is the ultimate 'how long is a piece of string' question. But this way of living has sharpened the focus for me. I didn't value life as much before I was diagnosed with dementia. Not many of us do. We don't think death will happen to us, which is ridiculous, really. Some people think about death constantly – that they're going to get run over by a bus. For those people life must be one constant worry, and then on the other hand you have people who simply go through life and accept whatever is thrown at them: they just live. I was perhaps like that, but it's only when something big happens – an incident, an illness – that you just stop and think: 'Have I done everything I wanted to in life? What is there I still must do?' If only we were programmed to appreciate the minutiae of every day, if only we had old heads on young shoulders...

I've never understood why people see talking about death as morbid – it has always felt perfectly natural to me. Perhaps that's why I feel able to talk about it now.

I saw my first dead body when I was studying at college. I must have been eighteen at the time. I was in student digs then, renting the box room of a house owned by Doreen and Albert, an elderly couple who'd been hosting students for years as a way of making a bit of extra income to top up their state pensions. I got on well with Doreen. I enjoyed the way she looked after me, cooking me breakfast each morning – one sausage, one fried egg. Treats like that hadn't existed at home; instead I'd made excuses to get to school early with my flask of tea and a packed lunch I ate for breakfast.

I rarely stayed out late and was always happy to return to my digs and spend time chatting to Doreen and Albert. Doreen had a thick, Geordie accent and smiley eyes, whereas Albert was of a more grumpy disposition, fond of his favourite armchair. But it was a warm and happy home, one that was perfect for my first time away from my parents.

It was in the early hours of the morning that the sound of Doreen's voice cut through my sleep. She was saying Albert's name, gently at first, and then with more urgency. It was the panic in it that made me sit up in bed. A second later she called my name and I leapt up, opened my door and found her kneeling on the floor at Albert's side on the landing. I assumed at first that he had fallen in the bathroom, but then Doreen looked up at me, her usual sparkle replaced by fear. She was shaking him, desperate to rouse him, but there was no response. Albert lay still, unmoving, not breathing.

I'd never seen a dead body before, yet I wasn't frightened. I was perfectly calm. Doreen turned to me, helpless, the devastation not yet sinking into her skin.

I reached out and touched her shoulder, a hand where words were failing me, and I felt her fingertips respond to my touch.

'He doesn't look comfortable on the floor, does he?' I said. 'Shall we carry him back to bed, then maybe you should ring a doctor?'

Albert was, by then, a frail old man, his body wizened by life and decades of work in the motor factories of Coventry. When I reached down to lift him, his flesh visible where his blue-striped pyjama bottoms were askew, I could see that under his clothes he was in fact all skin and bones. I put my hand around one leg, and then the other, noting that he was cold to my touch and realising that he must have been lying there for some time.

'You take his arms,' I said, directing Doreen who was following my suggestions through shock more than anything, grateful perhaps to have someone there to take the lead.

Only as we started to lift, rigor mortis was already setting in. It was a strange thing to notice, how Albert's skin still moved under my fingertips as if he were still living and breathing, yet his joints locked firmly in place. He was the proverbial dead weight despite his thin frame. As carefully as we could, we carried him into the bedroom and settled his body back onto the bed. I expected, in my naivety, to smell death on him, or in the room after we had settled him down. I was not sure what it might smell like and so I sniffed the air, curiously, but all I smelt was old man.

As I stepped back, I noticed how peaceful he looked, his usual grumpy expression replaced with something much calmer than I had seen written on him in life. Doreen hugged and thanked me. I don't remember what happened immediately after that, or the order of events. I must have made tea and stayed with her until a doctor arrived and pronounced Albert dead. But I went to college as usual and told my friends what had happened. I was surprised by how shocked and disgusted they were that I had carried a dead body that morning, and so I instinctively knew to say no more.

To this day I do not know how, as an eighteen-year-old girl, I managed to stay so calm that morning. Death, even then, just seemed so natural to me. Albert was old and had been in bad health for some time. Though upsetting for Doreen, it was not a great tragedy that he died; his body had simply tired and closed down. It was, quite obviously, Albert's time to go.

When nature takes its course like that, it can feel hard to argue with. Not for the people who are left behind – of course, Doreen still had her grieving to do – but Albert was taken within moments, a massive heart attack per-haps meant that as quickly as he felt the pain, it was over. That, as many of us with life-limiting illness know, is a blessing when a long time stretches ahead of us with no view of the horizon, and yet no ability to look back. We continue on towards the sunset. But for Albert, light turned to darkness in a split second.

I know what I would prefer.

Surely, there was a time when we were more comfortable with people dying at home? Perhaps when people lived with three generations crammed into one home, or in communities that had no need to lock their front doors. Was it the creation of the NHS in 1948 that medicalised death, took it out of the home and into the hospital? The NHS's focus was not, after all, on helping people to die but on healing them. In fact, its founder Aneurin Bevan said he would 'rather be kept alive in the efficient, if cold, altruism of a large hospital than expire in a gush of sympathy in a small one'. This perhaps gives us an idea of the early philosophy of the NHS and the new hospitals that started to spring up over the decades, the focus on life being preserved, of every medical intervention being used until each was exhausted. There would have been so many patients who were truly grateful for these interventions, yet people kept dying – as they tend to – and so it feels strange to me that there was no focus on provision for them, or for making them comfortable.

Perhaps back then we had a greater sense of community, perhaps it was expected that when treatment failed, family would see the patient through to the end,

alongside the local GP or district nurse. But it was charities that stepped in to find out just what death looked
like in 1950s Britain, as it is charities now that fund
the good deaths of the dying. To this day hospices only
receive around 30 per cent of their funding via the government and the NHS; the rest is achieved through
fundraising and those charity shops dotted along our
high streets.

Before the explosion of hospices in the fifties and sixties,
the Marie Curie Memorial Foundation was primarily a
charity for women's cancers, but a survey commissioned
by the foundation and the Queen's Institute of District
Nursing in 1952 sought to discover how people were
dying in England and Wales.[2] More than 7,000 responses
came back from nearly 200 health authorities and the
results made for disturbing reading. Nurses described
patients dying abandoned and in agony in beds they were
too weak to change, with ulcers they were too sick to
care for, and some without the energy to feed themselves. There were little details in that survey that made
for heartbreaking reading, like the people who chose to
keep their pets alive with scraps of food they so desperately needed for themselves. Many who had reached the

---

[2] Joint National Cancer Survey Committee of the Marie Curie Memorial Foundation
and the Queen's Institute of District Nursing, *Report on a National Survey
Concerning Patients with Cancer Nursed at Home*, London: Marie Curie Memorial
Foundation, 1952.

end of life were relying on the charity of neighbours to come in and give them sustenance.

Before the NHS had been formed, people were condemned to a painful death simply because they could not afford the prescriptions for pain relief, but these people who were reaching their last days and weeks were dying in the same way because they were overlooked by society and, often, the medical profession. The report's conclusions made many recommendations, and chief among them was the provision of hospices for the dying. The mission of the Marie Curie Foundation was rewritten as a result of that report – to provide adequate hospice care for people with end-stage cancer. The first Marie Curie home was opened later that year, and over the next ten years nine more hospices were created in old buildings that the charity acquired, and later, as the fundraising began in earnest, in purpose-built properties.

A further report in 1960 by Glyn Hughes on behalf of the Gulbenkian Foundation found deficiencies in end-of-life care. He found nursing homes falling woefully short in caregiving and often neglectful of their patients. Hughes noted that there was 'a serious gap in the National Health Service with unanswered questions of where and by whom the elderly terminally ill would be cared for'.[3]

---

[3] Glyn Hughes, *Peace at Last: A survey of terminal care facilities in the United Kingdom*, Calouste Gulbenkian Foundation, London, 1960.

It doesn't feel as if much progress has been made when you think of the lack of funding hospices receive from the government today. There seems to be a huge burden on a service that so many of us will need to access at some point, and little appreciation of how the general public feel about hospice care. In the most recent Marie Curie report, commissioned in 2021, on the attitudes of the dying, three quarters of people believe that end-of-life care should be given equal priority by the NHS. There is clearly a huge disparity between what the public want and what the state provides.

The 2021 report, *Public Attitudes to Death and Dying in the UK*, is a fascinating insight into how public perception of death has changed since that original report in 1952. It found, for example, that 51 per cent of people don't think we talk enough about death and dying as a society. Interestingly, the vast majority of respondents to the survey (84 per cent) indicated that there was nothing to prevent them talking about dying, and over 70 per cent of people said they felt comfortable discussing the subject and felt it was important to do so to decrease the burden on family and friends when it came to their end-of-life care and carrying out their wishes. Yet that doesn't translate into people actually *having* these conversations; just 14 per cent of respondents reported having had these difficult chats with their loved ones.

It is strange to me that we don't like to talk about death. Why is that? Why was it that my college friends found the thought of me carrying dear old Albert's body so horrifying? Death is such a significant subject – in some ways the only subject. It is one of two experiences we all share – so why don't we focus on it more? As former palliative care doctor Kathryn Mannix says in her excellent book *With the End in Mind*, there are only two days in our lives that are less than twenty-four hours long – the day we are born and the day we die.

It is not like this in many other cultures. In Sweden, for example, *döstädning* is the name given to 'death cleaning', which is organising your belongings while you are alive so that those you love have less to do when you are gone. Experts in this field recommend that 'death cleaning' should start when you are sixty-five, which may feel incredibly young to us, but personally I think that planning for your death should be something we consider the moment we arrive in adulthood. After all, we plan financially for old age, and we plan to pay off our mortgage in the event of our death – in fact, most mortgage companies insist that we have such a policy. So if we can have those types of discussions, however abstract they might feel when you're just about to unpack the boxes in a new home, why not also think about how you want to be cared for, who by, where, whether you want medical interventions, whether you want to donate your organs, and what you want read or played at your funeral. There's nothing to stop you changing your mind as your views change.

Fifty eight per cent of respondents to a YouGov survey, published in 2019 and commissioned by the organisation Dignity in Dying,[4] disagreed that death and dying was a taboo subject for them, though in the focus group that accompanied the survey, participants shared the difficulties they had in discussing death and dying: 'They think that people do not want to raise the topic or hear about individuals' illnesses, as it leaves them with a "bad feeling", makes them feel "uncomfortable" and can cause upset,' the report states. However, those within the group who were living with advanced or terminal cancer found conversations about death 'liberating', useful and/or positive. Of those participants who did discuss death regularly, the subjects most commonly covered were the practicalities, including treatment, pain relief and funeral plans.

A Welsh study carried out in 2018 and published after the Covid pandemic[5] managed to get even closer

---

[4] *What Matters to Me: People living with terminal and advanced illness on end-of-life choices,* YouGov/Dignity in Dying, 19 November 2019, www.dignityindying.org.uk/wp-cont ent/uploads/What-matters-to-me-Dignity-in-Dying-Nov-2019.pdf

[5] Ishrat Islam, Annmarie Nelson et al., *Before the 2020 Pandemic: an observational study exploring public knowledge, attitudes, plans, and preferences towards death and end-of-life care in Wales,* BMC Palliative Care 20, article no. 116, 2021, bmcpalliatcare.biomedcentral. com/articles/10.1186/s12904-021-00806-2

to the reasons why people find talking about death so uncomfortable. Again, a large number of people (72 per cent) felt that as a society we do not talk about death and dying enough, and that we should shift towards demystifying death, with a more positive approach to encouraging conversation on the subject. The concerns that made these participants avoid the topic were 'fear of the unknown, experiencing distress and becoming a burden to the family'. The report cited a 'general lack of understanding of death and dying processes and participants' frustration at being unprepared'. It seems odd to me that so many people are longing to have this conversation, yet most still remain silent. Nearly 90 per cent of the respondents *felt* comfortable discussing issues around death, yet the percentage of people who *actually* had was just 3 per cent.

So what stops us Brits from talking about death? Again, the Welsh study cited the 'fear of hurting other people's feelings', not being able to 'find the right time to talk', and some respondents even admitted they didn't have friends or family members they felt they could talk to. Participants suggested that public health campaigns could 'normalise conversations on death', particularly TV, social media and using public platforms – I guess a little like I always have for dementia. They also admitted they would welcome GPs starting these conversations but were too aware of their doctors' time constraints and workload. Palliative care staff, who bear witness to death on a day-to-day basis and are at the very frontline of granting those at the end of their life a good exit, must surely have an excellent vocabulary when it comes to discussing dying, and I could imagine that speaking to them would give people great relief, particularly those who don't feel comfortable having those conversations with their loved ones. But it turns out that even the medical professionals might not be as comfortable talking about death as we believe.

During one of my talks to student nurses about living with dementia, I met a researcher who was focusing her Ph.D. studies on dying with it. Catherine Wood graduated from her master's degree in Dementia Studies at Hull University. Interestingly, this course is the only one that has a specific module for end-of-life care for those living with dementia. Catherine worked in palliative care in hospices for more than twenty years before completing her master's, and for that reason decided to dedicate her Ph.D. to conversations on death and dying for those living with dementia. But when my co-author Anna and I met to speak with her, Catherine explained that even in hospices, nursing staff were often still reluctant to talk about death. I started by asking her why she thought there was such a great discrepancy between those who want to talk about death and those who actually do talk about it.

'I think nobody wants to talk about death and dying because they don't want to face their own mortality, or that of a loved one,' Catherine explained. 'It's so much easier to put that subject in a box, shut it and keep it away until you actually need to talk about it, which is often far too late. In care homes particularly, they have the tools to be able to have those discussions with residents, but in the event, they often don't have them because it's a such a complicated and complex topic and their staff don't feel they have the confidence to be able to take it on.'

I found it incredible to think that even the people who work in an end-of-life care setting don't have the confidence to start those conversations.

'I even spoke to my staff in the hospice, and said, "If you can't have that conversation about death and dying, who can? Because you are here, doing it every day."' Catherine said. 'But people would still back away from having that conversation. It is probably one of the most taboo subjects to talk about, and I don't know whether it's because people feel you might upset patients or you might offend them, but people just generally don't want to talk about it. If you don't have these conversations, then you are unable to meet people's needs at the end of life. There is evidence which suggests that anxiety – and particularly death anxiety – increases as you approach the end of the your life, and certainly with cancer, if people approach the end of their life and they haven't talked about what it is they want to happen, you see distress and restlessness increasing. It's called terminal agitation.'

Catherine told me about a friend of hers who had actually been a nurse at the hospice, and as she died, even though in life she had been surrounded by death, she was extremely agitated in her last few days.

'It seemed so unfair for one of our own to be dying in this way, and I knew we should be able to do this better for her — we owed her,' Catherine said. 'I remembered then a conversation we'd had once, when she'd told me that she liked listening to Classic FM, and so we put it on in her room and she instantly calmed.'

They wouldn't have been able to do that for her if they hadn't had the conversation. Something as simple as playing someone's favourite radio channel is not costly; it is a small act that makes a big difference.

'But if nobody had ever had those conversations with them, they would never know. Instead, people's families are then having to make decisions on behalf of that person, and it's stressful enough when you're at the end of life with a loved one. I've seen people arguing over the bed of a person who was dying, one person saying, "This is what Mum wanted,' and another saying, "No, this is what she wanted." What a thing to die to, hearing your family arguing over the top of you.'

And it isn't just for the sake of the person dying that those conversations are better had in the weeks and months, or even years that precede a death. To know you have given someone the death they would wish for must surely help those who are left behind, grieving.

Catherine agreed: 'Guilt is a huge thing after somebody dies and if you can't get over that guilt, it causes all sorts of problems, but if you know that you've done a good job for someone and you've been able to meet those wishes, then the guilt isn't too bad and the grief process, although always complicated, is generally more smooth.'

The conclusion of almost all recent studies seems to be that the general public are ready to talk about death; that it shouldn't be the taboo topic that it is. We have an idea that to talk about death is morbid, that it will hasten our arrival at its station, but as someone said to me the other day – and it will not surprise you to know that I cannot remember who – talking about sex does not make you pregnant, so talking about death will not make you die.

In 2011, Jon Underwood recognised there was a need for people to talk about death, and he founded the first UK 'Death Cafe', which he held in his home in Hackney, east London. Jon was a devout Buddhist and believed that people should talk about death and dying every day. The original objective of Death Cafes was to increase awareness of dying with a view to helping people make the most of their finite lives, and since its incarnation, there have been more than 14,455 Death Cafes held in eighty-two countries. The first Death Cafe offered tea and cake and a place for people to explore their feelings on death and dying. Yet Jon's own story came to a tragic and premature ending when he was diagnosed with a rare form of cancer that induced a brain haemorrhage, and he died suddenly in 2017 at the age of just forty-four. His mother, Susan Barsky Reid, and his sister, Jools, took up the mantle and have been running Death Cafes ever since. I was keen to know from Susan whether, in her experience, people were afraid of talking about dying.

'Some people are afraid, and some people just want nothing to do with the subject and think it's a really weird thing to talk about and don't want to think about it,' Susan told us when we met. 'I can't think of one Death Cafe that I've been to where people haven't laughed at one time or another, because it can be really funny and it can be really fun, and likewise, sometimes it's sad and people talk about the death of loved ones or a bad experience, or their forthcoming death, but I wouldn't say it's morbid. It can be sad, but that's a different thing. At the beginning, the Death Cafes used to attract a lot of people from the death and dying industry, and I can remember one where there was a lot of talk about what happens to the bodies in the crematoriums. Another woman came who made shrouds and she talked about how she tested them, but that was a few years ago and that was quite morbid.

'After Jon died, I stopped attending Death Cafes for quite a long time. I've been to just three since 2017, but the last one was last Sunday. I did one at my synagogue: one person there had a terminal illness; one person was a doctor; there were two men and five women. It's usually women who want to come, as it's always easier for them to talk.'

Susan told us about how Jon insisted on talking to her about Buddhist death rituals before he even became ill, and that she, like many people, dismissed him at first, finding the conversation an uncomfortable one. Buddhists believe that the spirit should be allowed to leave gently via the crown of the head, and some traditions facilitate this departure by tapping that area in a specific way. Jon asked his mother if she would do this for him in the event of his death.

'He said it more than once – two or three times,' Susan told us. 'And he said it to me, not his wife, or his sister. I used to say, "But Jon, I'm going to die before you," and he said, "But just in case, I need you to know this." And I did that for him after his death, touching his head in exactly the way he had described to me.'

Just like Susan, as a mother, I could not imagine my child insisting on having that conversation with me; it goes against the natural order of things to contemplate our children dying before us. But I could imagine how comforting it must have been for Jon that his mum listened, despite her protests, and I could see how that would have allowed not only him, but those around him, a better death, knowing they had carried out his wishes. Susan admitted, though, that she still finds it really hard to have those conversations with her other two children.

'I try and have these conversations about my own death,' she says, 'but your close family don't want to listen, do they? My children don't want to think about me dying because they don't want to think about the world without me in it, and I can understand why. It's like I didn't want Jon to tell me about that thing because I didn't want to think of the world without him in it.'

I feel incredibly lucky that my own daughters will listen to me when I talk about death. They might not agree with what I'm saying or want to hear it, but they'll listen, and I feel that's such a wonderful gift to bestow on someone, just to allow them to be heard. It seems to me that if you're not heard, then all you do is bottle things up in your own mind, particularly if you are facing or contemplating the end of your life. You could write things down for people, but you would never be sure they would read it; talking allows you to take in someone's expressions, to respond accordingly, and the two-way conversation is important, because it allows them a chance to say if they disagree, for you to hear their reasons, to find a compromise. Being able to have these conversations makes death, for me, more relaxing.

That seems like such a strange word to use, but I feel calmer for talking about death; it means I can let go of everything I want to say.

Perhaps, as a family, we're unusual. Maybe we have felt comfortable discussing death because for me it has always been a part of life. I was always quite open about death with the girls when they were young, explaining that eventually everything and everyone dies. I didn't tell them stories about heaven or stars or anything, although I understand why others comfort themselves with these thoughts. I remember telling them when my mum had cancer that the doctors would do everything they could to get it out, but sometimes it wasn't possible and it wouldn't be fair on Nanna to live long with that in her body, causing her pain. Yet I don't remember being as open with my own parents. In fact, I don't ever remember us talking about death before it came for them.

It's strange what we remember and what we forget; even stranger with a disease like dementia in tow, I can assure you. I don't remember Mum being diagnosed with cancer but remember everything else in fine detail right up to her funeral.

Dad had kept Mum's ashes in a box at the bottom of his wardrobe for months, and it was me who suggested we plant a tree and scatter her at the bottom of it – all these rituals we rely on to help us through the darkest times.

With Dad, I remember his diagnosis of lung cancer. I remember his phone call to tell me the news, his voice trying to sound very matter-of-fact – *too* matter-of-fact – the tremble in it was the giveaway. The next thing I remember is visiting him somewhere. I'm not sure where – this particular memory is woolly in detail, but it wasn't at home – perhaps it was a hospital, or a hospice? Perhaps I don't remember too well because the man I knew had been whittled down to skin and bones. Sitting in the chair beside me, the only clue that it was him was his Brylcreem quiff, still in place. That was the dad I knew and loved.

When the doctor came in, Dad struggled to stand out of reverence for someone he viewed as his superior, with his god-like status, this keeper of life and death. I can remember tiny details like the fact that as he stood, his nicotine-stained fingers reached for his trousers to stop them falling down; he had lost so much weight. I can clearly remember the words that came from his mouth. They fell, almost in slow motion, from his lips.

'Can't you give me something to end it all?' he begged.

I'd had no idea he felt that way.

I found myself in that moment's pause willing the doctor to say yes, not because I wanted Dad to die – far from it – but I could sense the desperation that he felt. I respected that it was Dad's decision and I was prepared to be party to this life-taking if that was what he wanted. Perhaps, now I think about it, it would have been 'life-saving' – saving him from a life that he didn't want, saving him from the man who would soon stare back from the mirror, a man he did not recognise. Saving him from suffering.

By then, Mum had already gone, and he'd seen just what the cancer had done to her and hadn't wanted the same prolonged ending for himself. It broke my heart that he did not have the right to choose that for himself. By then he was tired, ravaged by the cancer that was claiming him; he just wanted to be with her again – or at least that's how he saw it.

Dad stared at the doctor pleadingly, desperation in his eyes, and the doctor replied simply: 'I can't do that.'

It was as if a door had slammed shut on him.

They say that opposites attract, and that was definitely the case for my parents. Dad was a calm and gentle soul with a smile for everyone; Mum was more feisty, more ready to face her battles in life with sleeves rolled up, prepared to fight.

Perhaps I remember less of Mum's diagnosis because at the time I was a busy mum to my two young daughters, Sarah and Gemma, my marriage was on the rocks and fighting for that alone felt all-consuming. It is the only reason I can think for me not remembering such a devastating moment in our family life. I visited home with the girls often. I had no car then, so we would all pile onto the train and make an adventure of it. My parents loved to see the girls running around their bungalow. It had also been my home from the age of six and so I was familiar with every square inch of its floorplan, the sitting room crammed with all of Mum's little trinkets, many won each year on the bingo at Blackpool, and the clocks of all different shapes and sizes – the cuckoo clock in the kitchen being the girls' favourite. Mum was having treatment then for the cancer that had invaded her lungs, her stomach, even her eyes, but the presence of the girls took the shadow of death from my parents' shoulders: they remembered life. It couldn't have been more apparent, watching two toddlers race around.

The next morning, as I came out of the bedroom, the girls squabbling behind me on the bed we had shared that previous night, I settled on a stool in the kitchen and glanced through into the Anaglypta-papered hallway. The bathroom door was ajar and through the reflection in the mirror, I glimpsed a figure inside. I remembered that bathroom being fitted when I was a girl, and Mum's insistence that she wanted a coloured suite, which felt a novelty in the sixties compared with the dull, white cisterns that were de rigueur. Yet Mum looked pale beside her salmon-pink bathroom. Even the purple rinse in her hair seemed to have lost its usual glow. Mum couldn't see me watching her as she changed the dressing on the eye she had lost, a routine she had each morning before covering it again with an eyepatch, but in that moment, I saw for myself just what the cancer was taking from her. She looked old and frail all of a sudden, more vulnerable than she did in clothes. In that intimate moment, when she didn't realise anyone was watching, I could see the true toll the surgeon's knife had taken. All of a sudden, I felt like an intruder. I looked away quickly, leaving her to this private moment, but wishing there was something – anything – I could do to help.

Later that day, I took the girls to town to give my parents a break from their incessant chatter. Into my bag I had slipped Mum's brown tortoiseshell spectacles. I had noticed she hadn't been wearing them since the op. I guessed she felt there was no point trying to see, but I didn't understand why the one good eye she had left should suffer too. I promised the girls comics, then, after a trip to the newsagent's, I sat them on a bench in the optician's. I explained the problem to the optician, confiding in him about Mum's eye cancer and the operation. I handed him her glasses and asked if there was anything he could do to help.

'Is there any way to make these fit and useable just for the right eye?' I asked. 'Mum used to love reading the newspaper every day.'

'One moment,' he said, disappearing into his workshop.

He emerged soon after with a pair of glasses. He had cut them in half, yet left the bridge, which he had filed down until the edges were completely smooth.

'This should keep the glasses in place,' he said, 'but bring them back if they don't work and I'll have another think.'

We headed back to my parents' bungalow, the girls excited to tip open their shopping bags and discover the extra sweets hidden inside – all thanks to the coins Dad had slipped into my hands as we left.

'We've also got a surprise for Nanna, haven't we?' I said, fishing the adapted spectacles from my bag and handing them to Mum.

I told her the story of the how the optician wanted to help her and as I spoke, I saw her one remaining eye well with tears, particularly when I slipped that day's newspaper onto her lap.

As the weeks and months marched on, Mum grew more weary, but also more frightened. She had decided to make my childhood bedroom the room in which she now slept, and I would sit with her each night in the yellow-and-white wallpapered room, holding her hand as she begged me not to leave. Mum was afraid of falling asleep in case she didn't see the next day's dawn, not realising her fight was with herself, not death. Sleeping in the day felt less of a threat for her. So in the darkness we would chat about anything, anything but the cancer, anything but the impending end. When a lull fell in our whispered conversation, I could see her thoughts returning to death. I could see the fear resurface as the clocks ticked softly through the house.

How I wish I had known then what I do now; how I wish I could have told her that if she was still capable of expressing those thoughts, she hadn't reached the end. How I wish I could have gifted peace to her so that she might have relaxed into them; how I wish I could have told her that her breath was still steady, that it was safe to sleep, that she needed to sleep to conserve her energy for the things she enjoyed, like watching the girls play. But then hindsight is a wonderful thing. Back then, little Sarah had yet to become a palliative care nurse, I had yet to be diagnosed with dementia or to learn what the end looked like for so many people, or read about the pattern death takes, or how to make it more comfortable. I was in my early thirties and didn't know how to ease my mum's fears, or even get her to talk about them.

It transpired, in fact, that she had months left to live – all those months and months of energy wasted on fear, so much life left to be lived that instead she let slip through her fingers. Is this why I am the way I am now – because I watched my mother waste so many moments that were still bursting with life because she was so focused on death? I always say that dementia has a beginning, a middle and an end, but I wasn't able then to help my mum decipher the same about her own disease. I couldn't reassure Mum she would wake every morning because I didn't know myself.

I was there the day that the doctor visited my mum and suggested she move to the local hospice.

'So that's it, then?' she said, the clarity apparent in every syllable.

The doctor didn't say anything in response, and so she scanned him for some clue that he knew for sure that the battle, as she saw it, had been lost. She wanted to know how long – I know she did – but she didn't ask.

The thought of moving to the hospice did feel like an ending, though; it felt like we were all giving up, not just Mum. But hospices are, still today, such misunderstood places of care. I thought, like many still do, that hospices are just for the dying; I didn't realise that they were also a calm and clinical setting for someone with a life-limiting condition, a place they can go for pain relief, for respite or counselling, to be looked after, to recuperate enough to come home and live another day, another week, another month.

We took Mum ourselves to the Prince of Wales Hospice. It was situated in Halfpenny Lane in Pontefract, not far from the junior school where I played badminton, so the streets felt to me like returning home – I wonder if Mum had that sense too? I'd never been inside a hospice; I didn't know what to expect. Dad, Sarah and Gemma came too, to make the day more 'normal', an ordinary family day out. It was a single-storey building with immaculate gardens both front and back. We were told as we were shown around that many who'd had relatives here had stayed on as volunteer gardeners, pushing an extra tenderness into the soil, planting new shoots to spring from the earth – a permanent reminder that life goes on.

Inside the hospice, there was no rush; everyone had time – or made time – to stop and smile and say hello, as if they were suddenly more aware of the importance of a greeting gesture in a place where many came to say goodbye. The first impression was one of peace and calm, and flowers – flowers everywhere, and a huge lounge filled with comfortable chairs and stacked with books. The Sister took the girls off to find them a movie to watch, then came back to Mum.

'Would you like to see your room, Violet?'

She took Mum's arm while Dad and I followed close behind. We were shown to a bright and airy room. A pair of net curtains was billowing gently at one of the French doors, which was open, revealing the gardens just beyond the glass and the gentle hum of a lawnmower somewhere on the other side of the grounds.

'Oh Mum, this is like a hotel room,' I said, noting the crisp white linen and en-suite bathroom. It was only the single hospital bed that was the giveaway, with its cold metal sides.

The Sister offered to bring Mum some flowers and some magazines, but I could see from Mum's face that she was determined that no small gesture, no tiny attempt to divert attention could pull her focus away from why she was there – Mum knew she had come to die, even if she wouldn't say it. We busied ourselves unpacking bags and putting Mum's clothes away, and a few minutes later an auxiliary nurse arrived with a menu. Mum was instantly illuminated; she had always loved her food, and after a lifetime of cooking meals for her family, it must have seemed like quite a luxury to have someone asking you to choose what you'd like to eat for dinner. I think that won her over.

The girls came back, finally, Mum sitting up in bed, all of us beside her. The girls whizzed around the room, they simply *must* use the toilet in the en-suite, they *had* to open every drawer in the wardrobe, they *needed* to keep popping out of the French doors. Mum laughed, grateful for the normality that children bring, finding joy in the everyday moments we adults can too often take for granted.

I don't remember if Mum ever returned home, but I do remember she spent months in the hospice before she took her final breath. All that time wasted waiting for death to knock on the door: ready to greet it, everything in order, bags packed, waiting, all those moments lost for ever that could have been lived in.

There were special moments in that time, but they were just those: moments, pockets of time. There were more occasions when she was sad or fearful, or angry with Dad because he kept popping out for a cigarette. But then, looking back, maybe that was the drugs robbing us of the mum we knew, morphing her into someone we no longer recognised, with a quick temper and harsh words. But then that temper was probably the frustration of all those thoughts and feelings locked inside, all those questions she desperately wanted answers to: When will I die? Will it take a long time? Will it be painful?

We were called many times to say the end was near, but the out-breath continued to be followed by a breath in. It was typical Mum that when the end itself came, she was all alone. I asked the nurses if I could see her one final time; they led me into the room where she had been prepared for the undertakers. There was a chill in the air. I reached for her hand, but it was cold. She was still wearing her wedding ring.

'Do you want to remove it?' the nurse asked.

I was shaking as I tried to prise it away, the ring refusing to be parted from her.

'I don't want to hurt her,' I said.

A small voice in that huge room where the end had finally come.

It struck me when talking to Susan Barsky Reid about her son Jon and the Death Cafes he set up, that those who are attending them are distinct from the rest of the population because they are not only ready to talk about death, but willing and able. I wondered perhaps if these Death Cafes might be filled with people like me, those who face a diagnosis of a life-limiting illness with positivity, with an attitude of making the most of every day. I imagined they might be a vital and vibrant place to be, where people are released from the shackles of believing the topic off-limits. The conversations must be quite empowering.

There was, I realised, only one way to find out, which was to attend one of the Death Cafes myself. There were none happening near me, and so I made the decision to join one online in Kent. In hindsight, perhaps this was not the best idea – so much is lost in that great ether of the internet. Would it be possible to discuss such an emotive subject in the same way that you would if you were able to look another human directly in the eye?

I joined a group online one evening, which isn't the ideal time of day for me, as my batteries are usually running low by then, the cotton wool in my head thickening as day turns into night. The organiser of the meeting started by announcing that someone she knew had died suddenly that week while she was on a skiing holiday. Her shock and sadness were palpable, even through the medium of our Zoom call, and it rather set the tone for the rest of the meeting. How would it be possible to have a positive conversation about death if our group leader had recently experienced such loss? The organiser said that she wasn't sure why she felt surprised at hearing of her friend's death when 'it was bound to happen sometime'. I mooted that it was perhaps because it had been particularly sudden, but her sadness seemed to weep into every pixel, each little box that we sat within on the screen like a particularly sorry episode of *Celebrity Squares*. Someone else started talking and I shuffled up in my seat, hoping they might breathe some air into this virtual room.

'I feel that I am in denial that my ninety-nine-year-old mother is going to die someday,' she started.

I felt unsure how to respond to that. Ninety-nine to me felt like a huge number, a long life lived and worthy of celebration. Another woman who could only have been in her twenties said she was terrified of death.

'I just need to hear something positive about it,' she said, desperation cutting through the airwaves.

I mentioned that I haven't a clue of the dates that my mother and father died, and so I always celebrate them on their birthdays, a day which feels alive with memories.

'I've never heard of that before,' the organiser said sadly, mentioning her friend again.

I had been looking at my advance care plan in readiness for writing the next chapter of this book, and so that moment seemed a good time to bring it up. An advance care plan can be made at any stage of life, whether you are in good health or not, and it can be made up of all sorts of bits of paperwork that I will explain more about later, but broadly speaking it indicates your future care wishes should you be incapacitated, or in the event of being unable to speak for yourself. It struck me that if these people, young and old, wanted to talk about death, I wondered how many of them already had paperwork in place.

'The problem is,' I said, 'that the process of planning for death is so complicated that it puts people off having the conversation.'

I felt all eyes on me, an unvoiced question in the air that asked: What planning?

We moved on to the topic of sibling arguments. One person who had six brothers and sisters admitted that he had railroaded his siblings into doing as he thought fit rather than what his father had written down in his own advance wishes. He admitted with some sense of achievement that his siblings had just opted for an easy life, grateful perhaps that someone – anyone – was willing to take on the responsibility of decision-making and paperwork at such an emotional time.

An uncomfortable feeling was creeping over me that my dementia was quickly translating into sadness, as it tends to do these days, a roadblock in my mind preventing any more complex emotions. I had thought this Death Cafe would feel like attending an advanced

Spanish class, but I had found it full of beginners still grappling with trying to commit 'hello' and 'goodbye' to memory. I tried a few more times to make light of things, but my smiles and attempted jokes were met with sadness and the organiser's mournful references back to her dead friend. I was grateful when it was time to log off. I wouldn't like my experience to put anyone off attending a Death Cafe – after all, Susan had told us during our chat that often the meetings she ran were full of laughter.

For me, talking about death is a way of appreciating the present rather than residing in the impending doom.

Catherine Wood, who we met earlier, was planning on running some Death Cafes with people living with dementia as part of her Ph.D. research into whether those with dementia could talk about death and dying and record their wishes. I was keen to return to her to see how they had gone, in the hope that they had been more cheerful than the one I had attended. Catherine started by saying that she had to tell one of the tables off at her own Death Cafe because they were laughing so loudly. In a strange way, that sounded so much more like what I had been expecting.

'Several people had said they didn't want to come to my Death Cafe because they felt it would be too morbid,' Catherine told me. 'One of those people was a lady who came nonetheless, and on the day I looked around and she was smiling and chatting away. I realised then that I had given them an opportunity to actually articulate these things. There was one man there with quite severe dementia who couldn't really speak, so I wasn't expecting him to come along because people needed to have the capacity to sign the consent form, but obviously on the day I didn't want to turn him away. He came with his daughter and his son-in-law, and he immediately picked up the funeral Lego I had put out on the tables – Lego made up into coffins and things like that. We were able to communicate with him through the Lego, and his daughter was saying, "Oh Dad, do you like that?" pointing at the coffin inside a horse-drawn carriage. "Is that what you'd like for your funeral?" And he said yes.'

Catherine ran two cafes as part of her Ph.D. and told me how, at the second, participants had discussed a whole range of topics, from who they wanted to hold their hand when they died, to things like green or wood burials.

'One participant said to me: "I've never ever had the opportunity to think about this before, and never thought I could talk about it with other people, but actually talking about it in this group has made a real difference,"' Catherine said. 'I had a conversation with a carer and I'd said to her: "Why don't you have conversations like this with the residents of your care home?" and she said: "We just never complete the death and dying part of the assessment when people come in because we're too scared of upsetting everybody." But I think my Death Cafes showed that you *can* have these conversations with people who have dementia and, actually, they don't get upset, they don't get scared, they are able to talk it through and have fun.

'It was almost like I'd opened a door for them to walk through; they'd not had these conversations before because they were frightened of upsetting people. It doesn't have to be a miserable conversation – you can have a good laugh about it and know you've been able to achieve someone's wishes when they die and that lessens the guilt on those left behind. To have those conversations makes things so much better for the person and their carer.'

When Catherine said that it reminded me of a conversation I'd had with my daughters, how I told them I wanted my ashes to be scattered in two places: the Lake District and my beloved village. 'But you've got to make sure my legs are in the Lake District so they can walk around,' I told them.

It *is* possible to have these serious conversations and still have a giggle – in fact, that anecdote still makes us laugh now.

I have described the three deaths I have experienced in my life, and yet I am still left with so many questions about what my own might look like. I think back to the questions of the dying discovered by Professor Hinton in the sixties: How long would it take them to die? Would there be severe physical suffering? And would the suffering be relieved? As I write this, it is 2022 and these questions still remain unanswered for me – precisely because of our fear of talking about death and dying. I have the same questions and I have met many people in the course of researching this book who have similar questions. What follows is an investigation into what my own end might look like, and yes, what I would like it to look like if I were able to choose. What I know already, what I have stated in my other books, is that nothing is made worse by talking about it.

## 2

# CONVERSATIONS ON END-OF-LIFE CARE

When my daughter Gemma and her husband, Stuart, moved into their new house, the garden left a lot to be desired. The house was relatively new, so it wasn't overgrown with brambles. I could see that neat borders had been marked out in the recent past, but they had become riddled with weeds, and the plants among them looked uncared for and tired. Neither Gemma nor Stuart had a particular interest in gardening, nor the time in their busy lives to create and maintain a thriving outside space, but both enjoyed the results of my green fingers. I set to the garden with my secateurs, snipping away with the expertise of a hairdresser tidying an unwieldy head of hair, and before long, the garden began to take shape: hydrangeas that were once long and leggy with dried, brown stems were now neat and ready to burst into their large, blousy heads the following spring; a beautiful white climbing rose gave me images of a mass of white flowers running along the fence the next year as I pruned it back and secured its previously unruly thorned branches. My hoe nimbly weeded between each plant, revealing hidden gems along the way – a rock rose and ferns of all shades of green previously hidden among the tangle. On the back fence I discovered a sweet flowering jasmine and imagined Gemma and Stuart sitting back with a glass of wine after a long day at work, enjoying the last of the sun in their south-facing garden. I was delighted when I cut away the last of the weeds and found a solitary clematis flower beneath them all. I instantly recognised it as 'Nelly Moser', with its candy-striped petals, and so I carefully unknotted its delicate tendrils and tapped tiny tacks into the fence, weaving a trail of green garden string that it would be able to follow.

I enjoyed the hard work of pulling each weed from the earth and, with each one gone, witnessing the garden reveal itself to me. My enthusiasm for what might grow and thrive always outstripped the fatigue I felt after a couple of hours working in the soil, and yet this year it felt like the balance tipped on the scales. I would look out of the glass of my conservatory and see my borders choked with stray fronds, and realise that suddenly my own garden felt overwhelming. I realised with sadness I couldn't continue to maintain my daughter's too. It had been one of the last ways I had felt I was helpful to Gemma. Dementia has taken many things from me, and

I have had to learn to adapt to the new line it has forced me to walk, yet there was a reticence involved this time.

This was strange, really, when to be a mother is a constantly evolving role. Your adult child has no use for what it demanded from you as a newborn; your teenage offspring would be horrified if you wiped their nose as you had done when they were a toddler. So why was I so resentful of this particular stage of adaptation? I guess it is because none of us have children for them to have to care for us. The pictures we paint of parenting are always of us doing the heavy lifting of care. From the moment I was diagnosed, one thing that I was determined to hold on to was my identity as mother to my two daughters. For me, dementia would never be allowed to steal that: it was non-negotiable – I have been consistent in that thought and I remain so to this day. But as with all things in life, I have had to adapt alongside the disease. I cannot be useful to my daughters in the way I used to be or might hope to be ordinarily. I cannot run errands for them, or help them decorate, or walk the dog – all the little things other parents might enjoy doing to ease the burden of the busy lives of their offspring. But gardening I could manage – until I couldn't.

I asked on the village Facebook page if anyone knew of a gardener looking for work. This wonderful network managed to offer up someone to take over Gemma's borders, but he wasn't quite up to my standards (I might not have had the strength to do the task myself, but my supervision skills were still second to none!). Then a surprising turn of events took place. Unbeknown to me, Gemma had grown rather fond of this oasis I had created for her and had developed her own passion for learning more, scouring the internet for advice and schedules for what to do and when in the gardening year. I was walking past her house on one of my daily trundles when I noticed her front garden looking so bright and colourful, neat and transformed – exactly as I would have wanted it myself. I texted her to say so when I got home, perhaps just a little resentful that the gardener we had chosen had come through eventually, only for her to text back and say that it was all her own handiwork.

*I still need you to come to the garden centre with me and tell me what to buy*, she wrote.

I understand that need to hold on to the past, for things not to change, to avoid conversations with those we love that will inevitably flip the child–parent relationship on its head (believe me, I do), but there is a rite of passage to be made, a passing of the baton – or in our case, a trowel.

Why do we resist this exchanging of responsibilities when it is so natural? Nature seems to accept it without nostalgia: the hungry mouths of swallows in the nest will one day grow to feed their own young the same way. Like we pick our child up after a stumble as a toddler, wiping their grazed knee and sending them on their way, we later need to watch as they pick themselves up after devastating life events and dust themselves off – and that includes our own departure, though we won't be there to witness that. We'll just have to hope that we did a good enough job and equipped them with the tools to deal with it themselves. Just like the mums of those swallows.

I am proud that Gemma has discovered the same love of gardening that I have had my whole life. Our trips to the garden centre have replaced the ones we used to enjoy in John Lewis, only now we shop for plants, seeds and compost, not clothes. I feel useful again when I can advise Gemma on what soil is best for those perennials, or what to feed those annuals.

A burden is something I never wanted to become for my girls, but as this disease makes its march on me, I have had to ask myself how useful I can be to them now, and I know this is a question many of my friends living with dementia ask themselves too. Yes, I am a listening ear. Yes, I set alarms in my phone and iPad to remember to wish them a happy birthday, or to check whether today was a better day at work. Yes, we share many happy times, lovely walks, days out, laughs, and now we can add trips to the garden centre to that list. But my role as mother has changed with this disease, and those conversations we need to have together have taken on a new urgency.

None of these conversations have been easy to have with my daughters. When I was diagnosed with young-onset dementia at the age of fifty-eight, I had hoped those chats would be years away, but it feels to me a duty as a mother to navigate the fog of dementia, to cut through it and make my passing as gentle for them as possible, even if that means having difficult conversations now. I know my friends who also live with dementia feel the same, so it's likely to extend to people diagnosed with other chronic or life-limiting illnesses.

My friends Gail, George and Dory all contributed their thoughts to my second book, *What I Wish People Knew About Dementia*, and we enjoyed our Zoom get-togethers so much that afterwards we kept them going, nicknaming ourselves the 'Four Amigos' and releasing our recorded chats on our various blogs and George's YouTube channel. We saw our 'Four Amigo' chats as a way of helping others living with dementia feel less alone, and we hoped that if they saw us having what to them might feel like awkward conversations, they would have more confidence to have them themselves.

During one conversation, we turned to the topic of wills and end-of-life care, and at that time Gail (who was diagnosed with young-onset dementia at the age of fifty-four) was finding it particularly difficult to talk about 'the end'. In fact, she would probably go so far as to say she was in complete denial about the forward planning she might need to do, but, as she explains in this conversation, something changed. Perhaps when you have been diagnosed with a progressive illness, finding areas in your life where you can take control is surprisingly empowering, and she has also used humour to navigate those difficult conversations.

GAIL: You know that I had problems planning and discussing wills and end-of-life, but it was only after talking to you amigos that I suddenly changed my whole outlook on making a will and discussing the end. I just decided I needed to make it a more positive experience, so me and my hubby went to make our wills and it was actually quite jolly, quite uplifting. My daughter rang me just before we were going to the solicitor's and I said, 'I can't talk because we're going to make our wills,' and she said, 'How morbid,' and I said, 'No, this is something everybody should be doing—'

GEORGE: —this is where I decide how much money you get!

GAIL: *laughs* —and then I began to think, I'm actually in control of doing everything I want, and even in the solicitor's we were laughing and joking – we didn't make it a sombre occasion – and since then we've been more relaxed about talking about things. Just yesterday we were talking about my care and what I would want, and everybody in the family knows that I don't take drugs – all I've ever taken is paracetamol – so one big thing for me is that I don't want to be pumped full of drugs, because I just want to go naturally. So we were talking about care, and my hubby knows that I don't want to go into a home, and he said that he will do everything in his power to keep me from going into a home, even if he has to get somebody in to help look after me in this house. He said to me: 'Really, you'd like to interview the person who is going to care for you,' and I would, I'd like to know who's looking after me and whether we've got a good relationship, but I've got a lot to do yet, so it's a long time off, but we will plan things. We did have a bit of a discussion on whether I would want to be resuscitated or not, and I said: 'Well, that's a grey area, because at the moment I would want to be resuscitated, but that could change,' and hubby said: 'Well, I'm sorry, but I would resuscitate you whether you'd put yes or no,' and I said: 'Yes, but that's a little bit selfish.' But we're having the conversations now and it's not morbid – it's more uplifting.

GEORGE: It's interesting because I had quite a good talk with my wife two weeks ago, and we agreed that I wanted a humanist ceremony, preferably in our back garden – well, field – and probably scatter my ashes under one of the oaks there. But I said to her: 'If the children want a grave to visit, then you'll have to do something different,' and it's very much up to them. I don't care because I won't be here.

WENDY: I didn't want a service, but then Sarah said to me that having that celebration of my life would be part of the grieving process for her and that she would be missing out on that part if I went straight to the crematorium, and that made me change my mind and allow my daughters to have the funeral they want, because I won't be here. So in having that conversation we were able to compromise, to talk about how my decisions would impact on them, and because it would impact negatively on them, I changed them. It's a kind of reciprocal act of love to talk about death, to have those conversations; it's almost this dance between two people who don't know the steps, and it's no wonder that these are difficult conversations to have, but it just shows the power of conversation. If me and Sarah hadn't had that conversation, I was thinking I was doing them a favour, but in effect, by having the conversation, I realised I wasn't.

GEORGE: I do think the grieving process is a rite of passage which people need to have, which is why my initial reaction to the discussion with my wife is 'I don't care because I won't be here'. It's what they want.

WENDY: Gail, have you talked about your funeral or anything? Because I find it interesting what George is saying, that he thinks, *Well, do what you need to do, because I'm not going to be here*, but I'm also aware that lots of people do like to pick music and readings.

GAIL: Yes, we haven't written anything down because the solicitor said that sometimes the will doesn't get read out until after the funeral, which is too late, but my hubby will know what I want. I was actually joking about it at the weekend, because I went over to see my daughters and I can't mention anything about death to my girls because they get quite upset about it, so I decided to make it into a jokey thing, so I just said: 'As you know, I've been and made my will, and they asked have I thought about the music I would like,' and I saw their faces drop, and I said: 'I've picked one. It might not really fit a funeral, but it'll suit me,' and they said: 'Oh Mum, what have you picked?' and I said: '"Tragedy" by Steps, because we always danced to it when you were little, so we know all the moves.'

GEORGE: I thought that was by the Bee Gees.

GAIL: But Steps covered it too!

GEORGE: See, I knew I was right!

EVERYONE: *laughs*

It is incredible, when you allow people to talk about death, just how many people actually wish to. There is also a whole army of organisations out there who will aid you having those conversations. I had never heard of Death Cafes until we started writing this book, and likewise, I had never heard of death doulas either – though they prefer the term 'end-of-life doula'. However, it instantly made sense to me; after all, I had heard of birth doulas – those who assist birthing mothers – and I had often wondered why expectant parents are asked to write a birthing plan, and yet why are we never asked to write a 'dying plan'? This, it transpires, is one of the things that an end-of-life doula can help with. We met with Aly Dickinson, of End of Life Doula UK. Aly had had a long career in HR, though she jokes that people are happier to see her in her new role as end-of-life doula than they ever were as an HR manager.

It was, in fact, her own mother who, in part, inspired Aly to have this about-turn in her career. Her mother had died from cancer and both of her brothers received terminal diagnoses too. Aly describes her mum as being 'controlling in the best possible way'. When she knew she was dying, she decided she did not want treatment, was determined to hang on to choice and control, and planned her funeral to the nth degree. Aly felt that, as a result, her mother's death was a peaceful one, knowing that she was doing it the way she wanted to. So in 2014, when Aly read an article in the newspaper about end-of-life doulas, she knew that was what she wanted to do.

I immediately took to Aly when she told me that she had promised her clients that she would take care of their cats when they were gone – it just goes to show the importance of putting people's minds at rest before the end. Aly was keen to point out to me during our chat that an end-of-life doula's job is in no way medical, but it is practical, emotional and spiritual (whatever that might mean to the individual), from helping them get paperwork in order, to writing an advance care plan, or updating friends on their condition, or shopping and housework, as well as, sometimes, being there to hold the person's hand at the very end, and even preparing their body for the undertaker. Aly said that her organisation is often called upon to fill in the gaps in state care; for example, they often receive a call from a hospital discharge team about someone who wishes to spend their last few days at home. 'But really,' Aly says, 'once somebody does make contact with you, it's about focusing on the living that's left to do.'

I liked the sound of that, the emphasis put on making the most of the time left, even if that's just making a patient as comfortable as they possibly can be. There are currently 275 end-of-life doulas working in the UK, and all of them are trained, insured and DBS-checked. Aly is keen to point out that her job is about getting to know the patient as an individual. She says that sometimes, when there isn't a lot of time left, she has to do that very quickly, but there is also someone she has been helping for three years, and for people like this particular client it's about helping them to achieve any ambitions they have left and talking through how they want to spend their remaining time. Aly is obviously not someone who finds talking about death difficult, but she has been at the bedsides of many people who even in their last few days cannot speak openly about their wishes.

'Quite often family relationships aren't great and as doulas we have to go into that situation,' Aly explained when we met. 'Once, for example, there was a mum in a care home who was living with dementia, and she had two sons who were her attorneys on paper under her lasting power of attorney,[1] but it was clear they had never discussed her wishes. She felt very strongly that after her death she wanted to be taken from her home in the funeral cortège, but one of the sons thought it

---

[1] There are two types of lasting power of attorney (LPA) in the UK: health and welfare, and property and financial affairs. LPAs can be set up when a person is still in good health, or when they realise their health is declining, and are used when that person has lost capacity to look after their own affairs. An LPA authorises and registers someone else to make decisions on their behalf.

meant that she wanted to die at home, and the other was very anxious to get the house sold to pay for her care costs, so they both had differing views. The problem was made worse by the fact that the mother was telling each son what she thought he wanted to hear, rather than what she actually wanted, and so my job was to find out from her exactly what she wanted to happen and then bring all the parties together to focus on achieving that.'

I could see how somebody like Aly would be helpful to many families: those disagreements that are all too common are the reason I have insisted on having advance conversations with my daughters, but then of course a death doula is a paid service and that means it isn't necessarily available to everyone. But I was keen to hear from Aly how easy it is to talk about death with the dying, particularly how open – once someone has sought the help of a death doula – they are to talking about death.

'The way we start the relationship is to build absolute focus on that person and the way they lived,' Aly explained. 'It's not often people get that undivided attention. And also – what do you like and don't you like about what's happening to you now?

'The problems occur when there is a mismatch. Perhaps the parent wants to talk to their children about what they want and don't want, and the children are saying: "Don't be so morbid, we don't need to talk about this yet," and the parent might respect that, rather than gently coming back to it. Advance care planning can often be a way in, and I can say: "Let's all get together and talk about what it is that your mother is saying in this plan." Quite often people seem to be happier talking about the after-death bit, so they'll talk about funeral music, they'll talk about flowers, or the clothes they want people to wear, or the food, and you can work back from that and talk about the harder things like the "do not resuscitate" orders.'

The problem is that we never consider the prospect that we might have to care for somebody. People are just so unaware of what the future holds, and yet it's such a normal thing to talk about because the death rate for humans is still 100 per cent, so why is such little value placed on dying?

But with all this talk of death, what I really wanted to know was what it looked like to someone like Aly, someone who is surrounded by death every day of her working life, who holds people's hands as they get to the end. I asked Aly what death looked like to her.

'Just a fading away from this world,' Aly told me, 'just going away... going away... going away...'

Aly asked me if I ever tried to imagine dying, and I confessed that yes, I do, that I know it can actually be a peaceful process because of the different stages of dying – the difference in breathing, the difference in conscious state – which have made it sound less scary, unlike the dramatic depictions we see on TV and in films. People often talk of the act of dying, but to me it's not a physical act; it's more of a disappearing, a fading away, and that makes it sound so beautiful to me. It doesn't sound scary and horrific, full of pain or anxiety, because that's not what happens. Obviously you can have traumatic deaths, for example if you're run over by a bus, but you still have that unconscious state right at the end. It's peaceful rather than violent.

'Do you ever get that feeling when you're drifting off into sleep, that limbo land, and your head starts to go to all sorts of strange places?' Aly asked me. 'I love that feeling, and I imagine it's like that. I remember once working with a man with dementia. He wasn't focusing on what was around him as the end came, but he was focusing on something at the foot of his bed, and I just had an instinct that he could see somebody. My feeling was that he could see his mum, who was long dead, and so I put a photograph of her in his hands, and he died pretty quickly after that.'

It seemed to me such a beautiful thing to be able to understand death, and I know if more people had that understanding, they wouldn't fear it as much as they do. I can't remember now what I used to think about death before dementia, but so many people have this image of death as being painful. If they only understood the peaceful nature of how death comes about, they'd have a totally different image in their mind.

'It's almost something I'm looking forward to experiencing,' Aly said, 'if that doesn't sound strange. And I wish I could be articulate enough in that moment to come back quickly and say, "It's all right; I'm really liking this."'

Yes, wouldn't it be wonderful if you could give a quick thumbs-up, if you could say: 'It's good – don't worry, everyone!'

I loved chatting with Aly about death. It made me happy that we were able to find humour in these discussions, and it made me realise that if somebody chose to be surrounded by death in their day-to-day working life, was it really such a thing to be feared?

I know that it is the finality of death that frightens us, but it is also the lack of control that it brings with it, particularly for people who are living with chronic conditions, who may be wondering what the end might look like for them, as is the case with me. Could it be possible that some of this fear could be alleviated by talking about what the latter stages of their illness might look like, and planning now to make it more comfortable?

A 2017 study set out to ask the question what palliative care might look like in 2040 and who might need it.[2] The paper claimed that the number of people aged eighty-five and older who need palliative care will more than double in England and Wales by 2040, rising from 142,716 in 2014 to 300,910 in 2040. The steepest rise will be those who are living with dementia, whose care needs will increase almost fourfold. This makes immediate sense to me because so little money is being put into dementia research as I write this. The report points out that only a minority of those who need palliative care (14 per cent) actually receive it, yet deaths in older ages and the projected rise of chronic illnesses (*because* we have become so good at treating them, rather than despite) will drive this growth in the number of people requiring care. The report presented a stark warning: that to meet these demands, we need to start planning now. Yet successive governments do little to support their ageing populations, and if we can't talk about what a good death might look like, how can we work towards achieving it?

In terms of what people hope their own deaths might look like, Marie Curie's 2021 report, *Public Attitudes to Death and Dying in the UK*, gave some insights, with almost half of people (47 per cent) stating that their priority in their final days is to be pain-free. Forty-three per cent of people said being with their loved ones was of

[2] S. N. Etkind et al., 'How many people will need palliative care in 2040? Past trends, future projections and implications for services', *BMC Medicine*, May 2017, doi: 10.1186/s12916-017-0860-2, pubmed.ncbi.nlm.nih.gov/28514961/

the utmost importance, and for 35 per cent of people, being able to maintain personal dignity and self-respect was vital. There appears to be a drive within palliative care now for people being able to go home to die, but the report revealed that for those in their final years of life, being at home was their second highest priority, but for those in their final days, it was actually their fourth. Three quarters of people in their last years of life feared being helpless and dependent, with 68 per cent of people fearing pain and 56 per cent fearing leaving their loved ones.

People seem very clear about what they're concerned about and what they want the end to look like when they're asked and when they've had time to consider it, but how in practice do they relay that to their loved ones, and how important is it to feel heard as the curtain falls on the story of your life? Everyone I spoke to who works in palliative care agreed that those conversations were vital to peace for the dying and those left behind, but I wanted to hear more from those who had been through it. Was it really possible to make a painful process more palatable?

In 2018, Esther Ramsay-Jones went away with her husband and two children on a skiing holiday, but while they were there, her mother, Joyce, a former English teacher, suffered what appeared at first to be a stroke.

As she and her family rushed back from France, doctors discovered that her mother actually had a terminal brain tumour. Esther works as a psychologist in palliative care and, although her mother's diagnosis and later her prognosis were utterly devastating to the family, it seemed to me that there could be no one better placed to give Joyce a good death than her own daughter. Esther agreed to share her story with us, and I was keen to know how they had been able to navigate the conversations about end-of-life care at such an emotional time, and whether it was because of her work in palliative care that Esther was able to start conversations that might not usually occur between mother and daughter, or whether it was Esther's mum who brought them up.

'It was a combination, really,' Esther told me. 'We had always been quite a different family, really; we would often end up around the table having conversations about the finiteness of time and existence – it's probably why I ended up working in palliative care. Mum was really good at keeping me as a daughter and I felt I was being mothered by my mother almost to the end of her life. It makes me well up, remembering it, but I think that was an unbelievable gift. There was one occasion when she was clearly very, very ill, and I did not want to leave her, and she stroked my face and said: "You must go to your babies." I will never forget that. I think it showed huge generosity of spirit to be able to say in so many words, "I know people are going to go on without me."'

I was so blown away by this act of generosity from Esther's mum to her daughter – a mother herself – that she gave her permission to go, because of course, a mum would know that it would be good for her daughter to leave such an intense time.

'My mum had always wanted to live as long as she possibly could,' Esther recalled. 'I remember after she died, Dad found a note in one of her shoes and she'd written a list of five things she wanted to achieve. Number three was something like: "Live until I am eighty-five to see everybody grow," so she really did want to keep living. Her initial approach was to take as much treatment as she could as long as it wasn't going to put her into a worse situation. When a biopsy of the tumour confirmed it was a glioblastoma,[3] she didn't want to have surgery because the risks to her mobility and speech were massive, and as an English teacher, her vocabulary and being articulate mattered to her, but she did undergo chemotherapy and, a little later, palliative radiotherapy. But after the first ten weeks she shifted: she became much more stoic, much more accepting that she was going to die, and I think in many ways she had that refrain of not wanting to keep everybody waiting with her.'

---

[3] A fast-growing type of tumour that grows in the brain or spinal cord.

People can't be expected to stick with their initial reactions to being told their prognosis is terminal; they must be given time to let the news settle. I'm sure at first Esther's mum wanted to keep alive as long as possible for her family, as well as herself, to not leave her husband alone, for example. And people can't process all that in one go; it may need to happen over days, weeks or even months if you have time on your side.

'I think it takes an awfully long time to process those things,' Esther said, 'but Mum didn't have a great deal of time because she did die within four months of diagnosis. She said that she didn't want a funeral, that she wanted to be cremated – there's a mulberry tree in the back of Mum and Dad's garden and she'd had a mulberry tree in her childhood, so she wanted the ashes to be sprinkled around the base of that tree. She only wanted her immediate family there. She had always been a very able sibling and she decided when she was very poorly that she didn't really want to see her sisters, and that was something I remember thinking was a missed opportunity. But I think we just honoured where she was at, whenever and wherever she was at.'

I liked that idea: it felt very respectful of 'the patient'.

'This is a really strange way of looking at it,' Esther continued, 'but this is how I tend to see it, and it's to do with the process of mothering: when you have a newborn baby, they're in a state of absolute dependence and as a mother – or at least this was my approach – I was generally just responsive, trying to make sense of what my babies were communicating with me, and as far as I can see, that allows the baby to begin to develop a sense of his or herself in terms of a mind and a body. Personally, I think that is the process that one offers someone who is dying, particularly when they're struggling to communicate. You're still honouring whatever life force they have, whatever fragments of identity are left, as far as you can. So for me it's like the inverse process of looking after a newborn – how do you hold the hand of someone who is dying? For me, and I think my dad, her personhood – her essence of self – was of primary importance. So her being able to retain as many facets of her identity as possible was singularly the most important thing.'

I found this idea of personhood an interesting one, because just days before my meeting with Esther, I had been reflecting on how dementia was diluting my own idea of personhood, and it seemed to me that when there is no personhood, there is also no future. I see it all the time, particularly in care homes, after somebody with dementia goes 'over the edge', as I call it. People latch onto the happy moments, they'll see someone looking at photographs and think they're happy, or declare them happy in that moment, but they won't see the rest of the day, a day that might be spent in total confusion, not understanding why they're there, who these people are around them. That's not enough for me; my person-hood will have evaporated if I allow myself to become a person of moments. I'm not saying that everyone with dementia feels this way, but everyone with dementia has a right to life, to live in their moment; it's just the fact that I don't want to be that person. It's back to the person-centred acknowledgement of life, really, that – in my head – won't be a life if I lose the things that are important to me.

'That resonates with my experience with my mother,' Esther said. 'My mother did get to that stage. She had a very big seizure at one point and became unconscious and we thought we were saying goodbye. She did come back, but it wiped out her movement; she became bedbound, her speech had really disintegrated, and one of the most harrowing moments was her repeatedly saying: "Die, die, die." And I knew what she meant, that she wanted to die. And for me, from the outside, I could still see her personhood, I still saw how determined she was, but I don't think that was enough for her either, so she stopped eating, and it's hard to know whether it was due to losing her ability to swallow, or whether some-where in there she said to herself: "That's my way out."'

It perhaps feels strange for me to say, without knowing Esther's mother and only hearing her story second-hand, that I can fully appreciate everything that her mother was going through and how her thought processes were working.

'Of course I didn't want my mum to die,' Esther said, 'and I remember thinking: *Do I keep on encouraging her to eat, knowing that could become a pressure at that time in her life?* There was another incident where she had been fitting in the night and her arm was punching the wall, and she had in her advance directive "please don't let me go to hospital, or die in hospital", and we called an ambulance and the paramedics were lovely, but their job was to take people into hospital, and I just kept saying: "These are her words written down in her advance care plan. Is there anything that we can do here to make her more comfortable?" That was the only decision I made where I wonder, if she had gone into hospital would she have lived longer? But that was the terrible seizure she then came back from, and I think, actually, for me, having respected exactly what she had down in that care plan was the right thing to do. When she became conscious again, she was in her own home, she was in familiar territory, we could open the door and she could look at the garden. And when the paramedic left that night, he said to me: "I really want to thank you, and in a way I really want to thank your mum, because it's not often I get the time to really make sure that I'm doing exactly what the person who is unwell would want." Generally speaking, what I've been left with is that it's a loving act to let go of someone.'

I fully agree with Esther: grieving is made more stressful when you have to make all the decisions yourself, whereas just the simple things like: Do they want burying or cremating? can be incredibly stressful for people, but if they've got it written down, it causes less stress. Esther's mum was mothering her right up until her last breath, and that was part of her personhood too, identifying herself as a protective mother – exactly the same as I feel with my girls.

I found Esther's story so moving. It seemed to be a symbiotic act of love – Esther helping her mother hang on to her personhood and respecting her decisions, and Joyce's insistence that life would go on without her, that Esther should return to her children, knowing that they needed each other too, and like that, life continues.

Talking to Esther and hearing her story made my own wishes less fuzzy around the edges and come much more clearly into focus. To hear how she respected her mum's wishes made me feel more confident that all the conversations I've had with my girls have been for the right reasons, not only to have my thoughts respected, but to ease the burden of decision-making for them at an already difficult time, to make the grieving process that bit easier, because they would know they had done the right thing for me. I don't think there is a way of loving anyone more in this life than to grant them autonomy in death. Even though Esther works in palliative care, she admitted to us that no amount of professional training could have prepared her for her own dear mum's death, and I know that's something my daughter Sarah struggles with, switching between her nurse head and her daughter head. But then, perhaps, we all go through life playing different roles: mother, daughter, lover. What Esther told us about her mum releasing her from her bedside with thoughts of her own 'babies' resonated with me and every intuition I have had since being diagnosed with a progressive illness about how I don't want my daughters to care for me.

It was such a comfort to hear Esther speak of her mum's personhood, such an important topic for me in my own circumstances. Her mum, an eloquent word-smith, an English teacher, and the spoken word still such a huge part of her personhood after she'd retired.

As dementia dilutes my own personhood, I cling on to those things that make me who I am – a mum, a blogger, a walker and a photographer. For me, once those parts of me have been taken by this cruel disease, I'll have lost my personhood and would prefer death to an existence of snapshots of joy, as the time spent in confusion would far outnumber those moments. Esther had recognised that in her mother, and that had helped her to carry out her mum's wishes, whether she agreed with them or not.

Esther told us she was lucky to have such a wonderful mum, but I say her mum was lucky to have a daughter who accepted and listened. We often think of how making advance care decisions impacts those around us, those we love, but Esther's thoughtfulness even allowed the paramedic to make sure he was doing his job properly; it gave him 'permission' to go against his own protocol, to see the human behind the paperwork, even though at that stage Joyce was unable to speak for herself because she had suffered a massive seizure.

Whenever Esther spoke of the moments when she had honoured her mum's wishes, she paused and stared back into that moment of time, remembering the emotion, yes, but there was a calm in her expression, whereas when she spoke of the times when she had been forced to make a decision about her mother's care, the anguish was still there on her face, drawn like a giant question mark, asking still: 'Did I do the right thing?'

I couldn't help but think of my own daughters in those moments. As a mother – as I'm sure, just like Esther's mother – I would rather eliminate those question marks from their minds, stop them clouding their memories of me and replace them with the comfort of knowing that it's what Mum would have wanted.

I felt for Esther. Obviously, the loss was still there, but I felt I knew exactly the thought processes her mum had been through, and it gave me hope that my daughters could benefit from me releasing them from decision-making. No one wants to see their loved ones in turmoil, having to make stressful decisions at a time when life is already stressful enough. If I can reduce their anxiety in any way, I will. And more importantly, if it means disagreement is reduced, that makes me even happier.

I think the conversations throughout this chapter have reminded me of what a 'good death' looks like, the huge difference that can be made to end-of-life care when someone shares their wishes, how that can help them face the end with acceptance and trust that their loved ones can carry out their wishes, and that stressful decisions do not need to be made in highly emotive situations. If those conversations can take place, we know what palliative care can look like. So it seems to me that the more we are able to plan and share our wishes, the more chance we have of a better death. No matter how you look at this topic, it always comes back to the same thing for me, and that is personal choice, so we'd better look at that more closely.

# 3

# CONVERSATIONS ON REFUSING TREATMENT

It was time to speak with my daughters. The last time all this paperwork was strewn in front of us was almost nine years ago, just after I was diagnosed with dementia. Completing the lasting power of attorney was one of the first things my girls and I did after I got my head around the diagnosis. It had felt quite pressing then – if only I had known back in 2014 what life had in store for me.

I sweetened the conversation that afternoon back in 2014 with an afternoon tea of cakes I had baked specially, back when I could still use the oven. This time I bought cakes from our favourite tearooms in York; they were boxed and tied with gold ribbon, though I had not tied those neat bows myself, these days my fingers would get in a tangle trying to tie a bow, but as I have always said 'there is always a way' and so Betty's Tea Rooms came to the rescue.

It was a hot, sunny afternoon as I awaited my daughters' arrival, but that morning, despite the wonderful weather, the day had started in the haze of a thick fog, replicating the haziness and uncertainty I felt in my mind about how I would explain to the girls what was in my advance decision and why. They knew my wishes, of course, and so I wasn't expecting any surprise to them, but nonetheless, I still felt a great sense of responsibility in the way I described my advance decision to refuse treatment (ADRT) and what it now contained, particularly that I had committed to ink for the first time my wish to refuse to attend hospital as an inpatient, even if that decision would mean my life would be shortened. To be sure I explained this carefully, I had typed up exactly what I would say. Perhaps it was not nerves I felt as I waited for them both to arrive at the door, but a sense of trepidation – what mother would willingly have these conversations with her children? We know they have to be done, but it doesn't make it any easier...

At the time of my diagnosis, I couldn't focus on the future because I no longer knew what it might look like. I couldn't focus on the present, as it felt like I had too much to plan for – my future state, my care, my death. So when did all that change? When was the light shone once more on that four-letter word – hope? To begin with, it was when I took part in my first research study, trialling the drug minocycline, currently used for the treatment of acne and being repurposed in the hope of reducing inflammation on the brain for those with dementia. Taking part in research then, and even more so now, particularly that sense of redefining dementia in the future for others, gives me immense hope to this day. But personal hope was regained once I began to meet other people with dementia, when I first heard my now friend Agnes Houston standing on stage, speaking eloquently ten years after her own dementia diagnosis. Suddenly it dawned on me that I did have a future; I had the hope of following in someone else's footsteps, the hope that there was still a life to be lived, and the despair drained away. Once I regained my confidence, I found purpose in life. I found that it was me standing on the stage giving other people hope, and I knew that those who I'd given hope to would take the stage after me.

The only broken spoke in the wheel was that each time I went for an assessment, I would inevitably fail the mini mental test they set me. My scores reduced each time, even though outside of the hospital setting my confidence was soaring. Inside those four walls, all the medical consultants could focus on was how much worse I'd got. Where I was giving hope to others, the medics were snatching it away, and so I decided that they were doing me more harm than good; they were of no use to me. I knew only too well that dementia was taking little pieces out of me – I didn't need a doctor to tell me that: I was living it. My solution was simply to stop attending the assessments. That was in 2017, and I haven't had one since. It was such a negative process that any hope I had when I went into the room was diluted away by the time I came out again, and I am not alone.

So often among my friends who have been diagnosed with dementia, I have noticed that it is not the end of their lives they wish to discuss, but it has brought more sharply into focus the present. For that reason, many of them have also refused to attend their assessments and scans, not just because there is no cure for dementia, and therefore there is nothing that can be done to help – other than drugs which may, or may not, slow the pace of the disease – but because when you have a progressive illness the news is rarely good and they, like me, would rather focus on the day. After those assessments, it took a huge effort to remind myself each time that there was a beginning to this disease, a middle and also, yes, an end, but I had no idea where I was on that particular scale, and in many ways, if they could not cure me, did it really matter?

My friend Dory was diagnosed with dementia at the age of fifty-nine in 2012, but like me has stopped attending her assessments because she found they prevented her from living in the present. 'I would get quite depressed and upset when they told me that I had deteriorated,' Dory said. 'It was like getting a diagnosis all over again. I was thinking I was doing all right but I was obviously not doing as well as I thought I was. I've got to a stage where I'm quite happy in my own world, so do I really want to know I'm getting worse?'

Dory described to me the feeling of empowerment she has by making the decision not to attend the assessments any more. 'People like to remind me that dementia is progressive,' she said, 'but nobody knows in life what's going to happen – life itself is progressive – so you've got to live for every day. You may not reach that stage of progression – you might get hit by a car before that – so just live for the day. I feel I'm in control now, nobody's telling me I've got to go to these assessments where there is no upside, only bad news. You don't want to be told that you've progressed, and you probably know that anyway.'

Like me, Dory agrees that being diagnosed with a progressive illness focuses the mind on living.

'I don't think about my past. It wasn't a happy past, and I've put everything in place for my death and my care, so I don't think about my future either,' she said. 'I don't even think about tomorrow. If I'm happy today, I'm happy. And I'll take a risk too, if I want to do something I enjoy that maybe, if you were in a care setting, they wouldn't allow you to do. I'd rather die doing something I'm enjoying, not just die sitting in a chair in the corner of a care home.'

Everything that Dory said resonated with me; we certainly share the same philosophy, and, like me, Dory has had those important conversations with her children.

'I called a family meeting and told them to bring wine,' she told me. 'I got my future care plan out and they were saying: "Don't let's talk about that." But I insisted. I said to my son: "What would you do when I get to the stage when I can't manage on my own? What's your plan for me?" And he said: "Well, you'd have to go into a home, wouldn't you?" And my daughter said: "You'd have to come and live with us." But I told them that I didn't want them to end up looking after me, that they had their own families, their own children. It is important for me to be able to live my life and enjoy my life, knowing that my wishes will be carried out at the end. I've said that I don't want resuscitating; I want quality of life and control of my life.'

Dory insists that the reason she's forced her children to have these uncomfortable conversations now is so that she can get on with living and enjoying her life, knowing that her wishes will be carried out in the end. But even before you reach the end stages of an illness, many of us forget that we do have a right to question the treatment that doctors are suggesting, and that doesn't just mean the autonomy to stop attending assessments, but, in the case of other diseases, refusing treatment or surgery.

In 2016, the Academy of Medical Royal Colleges launched Choosing Wisely UK, which was part of a global initiative aimed at improving conversations between healthcare professionals and their patients.

The organisation developed a shared decision-making strategy with the acronym BRAN, which they recommended should be the bedrock of any consultation with regards to treatment or surgery by asking these four questions: What are the **B**enefits? What are the **R**isks? What are the **A**lternatives? And what if I do **N**othing?

You could apply this strategy to both large and small dilemmas: a consultation with your GP about whether you should take a vitamin-D supplement, or indeed major surgery and chemotherapy. It seems to me a very simple way of starting a conversation with a medical professional, rather than – which occurs all too often – simply accepting what they say should happen to you next, according to their own criteria.

In many ways, our health service wishes for us to be more proactive in decision-making (it empowers expectant mothers and asks them to write birthing plans, for example), and yet many of us still find resistance when we decide to step off the medical treadmill, as Dory and I did. But I wondered if perhaps that was just our experience of dementia, given that none of us could be offered a cure. I know that I, and my friends who have done this, feel a greater sense of control over our lives, our bodies and therefore, yes, our minds, these minds that are failing us in other areas. While we can still make decisions, we do. But I wanted to speak to others who lived with different conditions yet felt similarly.

Molly Bartlett was diagnosed with kidney cancer in 1999 when she was fifty-one. She had a right radical nephrectomy (when the surgeon removes the whole kidney and tissues surrounding it) and was left with only one kidney, but seven years ago doctors discovered two further tumours in her remaining kidney and one tumour on her adrenal gland. There were no treatments that would cure her, only those that would prolong her life, and all involved a life revolving around regular dialysis. At the time of Molly's second diagnosis, she had been looking forward to a summer free from hospital visits, as her partner, Helen, had just finished her treatment for breast cancer. This news came at a bad time for Molly, but the consultant diagnosing her assumed she would press ahead with any treatment they could offer. However, Molly didn't want to spend her life tied to a dialysis machine and sought a second opinion, which came up with the same scenario, and that got Molly thinking.

'I realised that I wanted quality of life over quantity,' she said when we met. 'But it wasn't that easy to get off the medical treadmill. I am a reasonably assertive individual, but I felt I might be persuaded the other way. The first doctors I saw didn't even question the possibility that I wouldn't have treatment – none of them said, 'Well, of course one option you have is to do nothing.''

In the end, Molly wrote a letter to her consultant and GP, who accepted her decision to refuse treatment, but seven years on from that diagnosis, Molly has noticed that she is in the minority among her peers at the hospice she attends for respite. It was interesting for me to meet a kindred spirit, someone who felt the same as me and my friends. I wanted to know more about the decisions she had made and the effect that had on her – after all, the last seven years of Molly's life could have been filled with hospital appointments, but as she sat chatting to Anna and me at home via a Zoom call, looking relaxed and happy and just in from the garden, it was hard to argue that that might have been a better option for her.

'I have met many people who just assume that what medics are saying is right and that you have no choice, and I have seen how their lives are full of scans, waiting for results and appointments with consultants,' Molly told me. 'But I decided not to do that. We know that the disease itself is not in our control, but taking some control in another way can feel therapeutic.'

This really resonated for me. I find it so important to be able to make decisions about my care now because I know there could come a time where I don't have control and the dementia progresses. If I don't catch it in time, then I've lost all control and I'm 100 per cent in other people's hands, which is where I don't want to be. I don't go to my assessments because, like Dory, I'm avoiding all the negativity, but I was keen to know if Molly felt the same.

'Yes, I feel exactly the same,' she said. 'You can listen and read your own body. My living is definitely scaled down from how it was, but I'm not preoccupied by that; in fact, I was talking to my partner only this weekend because I can't go on some lovely walks on the Downs, and we were pondering how well I'd do with my walker and whether it would be an assistance or not, or whether I should invest in one that has special wheels or something, but sometimes getting on with what you want to do is adjusting this way or that way to still maintain the pleasure. I happened to know Henry Allingham, who was a First World War veteran, and he was 113 when he died, and he said to me: "It's all about adjustment, my dear," and he was so right. Whatever life throws at you, it's your capacity as a human being to adjust.'

I know there will come a time when I've had enough of adjusting, as my brain takes away more of me, and I want it to be my choice that that's all right. Often it's other people who don't want you to give up, but for me it's just important I have that choice. My daughters are very tuned in with me and they accept everything; they might not agree with it, but they accept it because that makes such a difference. You don't then have that inner turmoil of thinking you're upsetting someone else; you don't have that battle in your head. It's a very lucky situation to be in, because that one act of kindness goes a long way to making the prospect of the last bit of life feel so much better and more peaceful.

I had so much in common with Molly – not least our mutual love of paperwork – and like me, she has many things in order already, but what we also both agreed on was the fact that the conversations we need to have with those we love must go hand in hand with the paperwork: you really cannot have one without the other. Which of them comes first – the conversation or the paperwork – is probably down to the individual. For example, if you're struggling to have the conversation, the paperwork might be a bit of an icebreaker, like it was for my friend Gail, who was finally able to talk to her daughters about death by telling them that she had an appointment to write her will. Other people may want to feel clearer about their own decisions and commit them to paper before they talk to loved ones. For some, the conversation must come before the paperwork, so it can be put together in full knowledge and agreement of their friends and family. I have been talking for three books now about the power of conversation, and it is still as vital as ever, particularly when it might mean – quite literally – the difference between life and death, or at least a good death. But it's not just communication between us and those we love that needs to be clear; we also need to communicate well with medical professionals – in this way, it is vital that we speak *their* language, because in the moment, it is their interpretation of what you have written in an advance care plan that will be most important.

Despite all the work I do in this area, despite all the tables I sit around, either physically or virtually these days, I still had questions about what my own death might look like. I thought again of the report carried out by Professor John Hinton in 1963, and the questions that the dying so desperately wanted answering: Will it take a long time? Will there be suffering? Can suffering be relieved? I had many of the same concerns, but who to ask?

Kathryn Mannix has spent her entire career working in palliative care. She started out working in cancer care but found that she could have the biggest impact working not with those who could be cured, but with those who couldn't. In the early nineties she trained as a cognitive behavioural therapist, and started the UK's first CBT clinic for those at the end of life to provide a safe space for people to ask the questions that they were so desperate to ask and to help them come to terms with the answers. Kathryn has since gone on to write the *Sunday Times* bestseller *With the End in Mind: How to Live and Die Well*, and *Listen: How to Find the Words for Tender Conversations*. As Kathryn tweeted in the summer of 2022: 'Medicine has advanced so much, saving people from early deaths. But the death rate is still 100 per cent.'

There seemed no better person than Kathryn, with her wealth of experience, to speak to about what death might look like for me. When I listened to her book *With the End in Mind*, it answered a lot of questions for me. There is a section about how, as a trainee, she observed a consultant at the hospice she was working at describing to a woman how she might meet death. The woman desperately wanted to know whether she had the courage to face it; she was afraid that it would be painful for her – just as those Professor Hinton questioned were concerned. Kathryn recounts how the consultant reassured his patient that if she had not experienced a great amount of pain thus far in her illness, it was unlikely that she would suddenly start to experience pain as the end arrived. Kathryn listened as the consultant described how, as patients get weaker, their experience in the final weeks, days and hours becomes very similar:

> As time goes by, people become more tired, more weary. They need to sleep more, to boost their energy levels ... what we expect to happen from now on is that you will just be progressively more tired, and you will need longer sleeps, and spend less time awake ... as time goes by, we find that people begin to spent more time sleeping, and some of that time they are more deeply asleep, they slip into a coma ... and so at the very end of life, a person is simply

unconscious all of the time ... the breathing slows down, and very gently stops. No sudden rush of pain at the end. No feeling of fading away. No panic. Just very, very peaceful...

I would imagine that this description would put many people's minds at rest, but we are too used to seeing dramatic, painful (or painfully acted) deaths on our TV and movie screens – no wonder we are terrified. But that particular consultant was describing a death from cancer, and I still had questions about what my own death might look like, and how people with dementia die.

'The way death is described in that particular part of my book is not really cancer dying,' Kathryn explained when we met, 'it's just dying. It's heart failure, liver failure, lungs falling apart – it all looks pretty much the same. There are things about dementia which we'll come on to, because bits of the brain fail earlier, but the pattern is the same. A hundred per cent of us are going to die, and almost all of us will do it through this kind of final, common pathway that the body does in the same way as any of us who've ever had a baby generally follow a common pathway of labour.

'There are patterns in the dementias, and one of the things is the interesting journey that people go on, often not the patients so much as the family realising this isn't just a memory problem, it's a whole-brain problem, and how amazing our brains are, how many bits of us – personality, mood and the bits of our body that are moved and controlled by the brain – can be interfered with by the short-circuiting that's going on.'

I addressed this in my second book, the challenges that we face when we are living with dementia, and of course it stands to reason that the short-circuiting also affects how we die with dementia.

'We know that one of the things that happens in dementia is that gradually the control of swallowing is lost,' Kathryn continues, 'and there's a really important decision to be made at that point in the illness, whether the point at which I lose my swallowing becomes the point at which I will no longer have food any more, and I would give permission for a feeding tube to be put in.'

Kathryn explained to me that a PEG tube (PEG stands for percutaneous endoscopic gastrostomy) can be installed via a tiny hole directly into the wall of a patient's abdomen and then into their stomach.

'You drip it through the night-time while the person is asleep; again, a bit of a challenge in dementia when people's sleep starts to go a bit haywire because, guess what, our brain manages our sleep cycles too. But there are some people who will make advance decisions to refuse that treatment on the basis that if I don't eat, I don't have to live into a protracted phase of further brain failure because I'll starve before that's happened, and there are palliative care protocols that help people not have the suffering that would go with the starving, like tummy cramps, so that they are helped to stay comfortable while they're dying. But what they're dying of is starving, but they're starving because their brain will no longer allow their throat to swallow, so they're dying of one of the effects of dementia. But we show people we love them by feeding them, so families feel very torn by the idea of not feeding them.'

I could see that this might be the case, but it is perhaps a good place to pause because I have already mentioned future care plans and advance care planning (ACP), and advance decisions or living wills, and maybe some of these terms need further explanation. I wrote in my first book that after I was diagnosed with dementia, I gave my daughters lasting power of attorney. This means at a time when I no longer have capacity, my daughters will be able to speak for me when it comes to health and financial matters – for example, accessing my bank accounts so they are able to pay household bills for me. This was one of the first pieces of paperwork that I put in place and, as I have explained in earlier sections, this allowed us to have conversations about advance care or funeral decisions. But, as I write this, that was eight years ago, and over the years I have added various different pieces of paperwork to the folder that contains my wishes, each one adding another layer of confusion.

At peer-support meetings or other conferences, I often heard people referring to advance decisions, future care plans, ReSPECT forms (ReSPECT stands for recommended summary plan for emergency care and treatment) and even advance care planning interchangeably, and even though much of my advocacy in dementia deals with all of this, I was still unsure what it all meant, which form was most important and, more vitally, did I have the right things in place to ensure that my wishes would be carried out?

Where do you even start to access this information? After all, no one from the medical world will prompt you to have these kinds of forms in place. Your GP will not be sending you a letter as a reminder and, equally, they will not carry out your wishes if there isn't any paperwork in place. It is like I've always said: you don't know what you don't know. And don't think this is only a consideration for those with a chronic or life-limiting illness; after all, someone in their twenties could get knocked unconscious by a bus tomorrow – and who would know what treatments that unconscious person would wish to endure unless they have written their wishes down or assigned an attorney to speak for them? Until we are sixteen, our parents will act in our best interests with advice from doctors, but there seems to be a great chasm between then and the last years of our life in terms of how those who love us would help doctors care for us if we were unable to speak for ourselves. This is not only a problem for the elderly or the infirm – it is a human problem; it is everyone's problem. But luckily, there are solutions.

We've talked about the importance of conversations with our loved ones so that they might be able to inform doctors of our wishes, but that will only ever be guidance to a professional unless it is committed to paper. I know paperwork is so, so boring – it feels dull to even be writing it down here for you – but it could be the difference between a good life and a bad life, quality of days and quantity of days, and a good death and a bad death, so it is vitally important that we know what is what, which documents are the most important, and which ones hold the power to enable those we love to act as we would hope they would. It's also not just about what you write, but how you write it. As Molly and I discussed, advance decisions are specifically for the medics, so you have to talk the medical language and that does put many people off doing one, because they don't think their GP has time to do that sort of stuff, or they're too embarrassed to go. It's no wonder that some people don't do anything – they haven't a clue what to do. It's all there for a purpose but the advance decisions has to be slick and precise: they're not going to read it if you waffle away. Fortunately, there are charities such as Compassion in Dying that do have the time and expertise to help you think through your wishes and translate them into an advance care plan that medics can understand and follow.

'I've got a great advance decision to refuse treatment. I'm really happy with it,' Molly said. 'I did it with my lovely consultant at the hospice and it's therefore constructed in terms that doctors can follow but is following what I would wish. We review it and have another look at it — I checked out that during Covid it would still hold tight to everything I wanted. But what concerns me is that the paperwork can be signed by anyone. I had the misapprehension that it had to be someone from the medical profession, but actually it doesn't. So you could have an ill-informed witness just willing to put their name to it, but I feel there must be a proper conversation so you get what you want, partly so it's written in a way others can follow, and partly so you get checked out a bit, in the sense that you're clear about over the decisions you have made, particularly considering how it is a legally binding and significant document.'

I absolutely agree with Molly, simply because I think the language on it has to be medical because otherwise medics might not be 100 per cent clear about what you want. Compassion in Dying therefore recommends everyone discusses their advance decision with their GP and ensures their surgery has a copy on record.

I put together my advance care plan six years ago with the help of my daughter Sarah, who is a nurse, and my GP, but only because I asked for an appointment with her to go through it. But since then, I have learned so much and my disease has progressed, and so, when writing this book, it seemed like a good time to revisit it. But who could possibly help me navigate this mountain of paperwork?

Clare Fuller from Speak for Me LPA has thirty years' experience working as a registered general nurse in palliative care in hospices, in hospitals and in the community, but it was only when navigating the paperwork for her own close relative in 2020 that Clare decided to set up her own business to help people with their own advance care planning, including writing lasting powers of attorney and advance decisions and to promote a better understanding among medical professionals of advance care planning.

'It is true that we need to normalise conversations about death and dying,' Clare told me when I met with her. 'But we also need to normalise conversations about planning ahead, so for me, I have done my lasting power of attorney because I don't know what might happen the next time I drive up the road. I work very hard at normalising these conversations that many people find scary, and that people tend to think is something you do in a panic at the end. All of us should be thinking about advance care planning.'

Clare agreed to work with me to make sure that all my own paperwork was in order, and through her guidance I understood better what I needed to have in place and, vitally, how to word it.

I explained to Clare during our first meeting that I kept hearing people refer to an 'advance care plan' but that I could not find a document entitled that among my own bundle.

'Healthcare professionals think there is an advance care plan, members of the public think there is an advance care plan, but there isn't an "advance care plan",' Clare explained. 'It could be an advance decision to refuse treatment, or your ReSPECT form, which says you do not wish to be resuscitated; it could be a lasting power of attorney; it could be organ donation, or a digital legacy (what happens to your social media accounts when you've died), or what happens to your pets.'

It felt so comforting to realise from the very start of our conversation that there was nothing that I was missing, that, as Clare says, there is no 'advance care plan', and no centralised system that it is logged in for medical professionals including paramedics, but there is advance care planning, which consists of all these documents. But where to start among them? And does one take precedence over another? It is no wonder that in January 2022 Clare started her own podcast series, *Conversations About Advance Care Planning*, which features a different guest on each episode talking about a different part of the process. What Clare is keen to impart is that this should be part of 'normal life planning' and I tend to agree with her – when we buy a house we are sold life insurance, which pays off the value of the mortgage in the event of our death, so shouldn't planning for our own healthcare be as common as that?

'You get reminded to have a breast check as a woman or a prostate check as a man – this is just normal life,' Clare says. 'We plan for where we go to school; we plan for university; we plan whether we want or don't want to have children by using contraception. If we're lucky, we get to plan our careers, and we often plan our funerals, but we don't plan for that bit in between. My argument is that we are all on this journey through life, we will all die at some point, and it's not a surprise to any of us – or it shouldn't be – so we should think about it. Advance care planning doesn't have to be all the "scary stuff" – it can be joy lists too.'

This is very true. In 2020, I received a copy of *My Future Care Handbook* from Zoe Harris, founder and CEO of MyCareMatters, a not-for-profit organisation. You may remember Dory mentioning her future care plan a few pages ago. It is a great resource where you can write many of your wishes down in terms of advance care planning, funeral and digital legacy. It is not a legal document but more of a conversation starter, something to help you and your family streamline your thoughts and wishes. Vitally, it also includes your likes and dislikes for any future carers; whether you prefer a nightie to pyjamas, how you like your tea, whether you prefer a shower or a bath, what radio channel you enjoy listening to, what you prefer to be called. We know that it is often the small things that give us the greatest joy, and so Clare is right: when future planning, we must pay as much attention to our joy lists as anything else, and even, as Aly said in the last chapter, our bucket list – the things we would like to do or achieve while we are still living.

Clare agreed to go through my paperwork with me as part of an audit of my advance care planning. She told me from the outset that one of her priorities was to make sure that we had checked through my own advance decision to refuse treatment, that I understood it and was happy with it. I asked Clare if this was the most important document, in her opinion.

'You could ask ten different people and get ten different answers,' she said. 'In many ways advance care planning is more about processes and conversations, and if you strip all of it away, you could say the most important thing you can do is have those conversations with your daughters, because if you were to lose capacity today going for a walk around your beloved duck pond and suffer a fall which knocked you unconscious, the most important document, I would argue, is your lasting power of attorney, because if you lose the ability today to say what you want, you have granted that ability to your children. But even that document itself is weak if you have not had the conversations that go hand in hand with it, because your daughters might not know how to answer any questions they may get from medical professionals.'

Clare told me that people often write their lasting power of attorney (LPA) and then tuck it away in a drawer without having the conversations that go along with it.

'It's a bit like having a building with no foundations,' she said. 'Those foundations are there to make that building stand up.'

This made perfect sense to me. LPA forms are available from the Office of the Public Guardian (www.gov.uk/gov ernment/organisations/office-of-the-public-guardian) and you can also fill them in online. There is guidance on how to complete the forms, but my advice would be to talk it through with someone like Clare to make sure that everything is in order for having it validated by the Office of the Public Guardian, as the wrong wording can see it refused. There are two types of LPA, one for health and welfare and one for property and financial affairs. You can choose to make one type or both. The health and welfare LPA only comes into practice once you lack mental capacity and you cannot make decisions for your-self, but, with your consent, the property and financial affairs LPA can come into practice once it's registered by the Office of the Public Guardian. You must be over eighteen and have mental capacity at the time of making your LPA. There is a cost involved in registering them with the Office of the Public Guardian – though some people may qualify to do this for free – and at the time of writing this book, it was £82 per LPA (there may also be further costs involved if you use an organisation or solicitor to help you fill in your forms; some charitable organisations do offer this for free from time to time). You can refer to the fact you have an advance decision in the LPA document, without going into the detail of what it contains, unless you wish to. Alongside this paperwork it's also very important to discuss what you have outlined in your advance decision with the people who you nominate as your attorneys, because, as Clare explained, how can they carry out your wishes if they don't know what they are? This all helps to empower your attorneys as much as possible, so they can advocate on your behalf with confidence, backed up by your written detailed wishes.

Clare checked both of my powers of attorney, particularly the health and welfare one, to ensure that I had granted my daughters the ability to make decisions about life-sustaining treatments. There is an option to only give your attorneys the power to make important healthcare decisions, but any life-sustaining treatment decisions would only be made by a healthcare professional, so that made little sense to me. If you have assigned two attorneys, there is also an option as to whether they should make decisions jointly or separately, and it is worth bearing in mind that if you decide they can only make decisions jointly and one attorney could not reach the other because they were on holiday, for example, they would be unable to make a decision in a medical emergency. Or in the unfortunate event of the premature death of one of your attorneys, your document would be null and void. There is no centralised system for any of the paperwork we are discussing on these pages, and so it will be down to your attorneys to keep a copy safe (or know where you keep yours) and show it to medics if and when necessary, though the Office of the Public Guardian does hold a copy of your documents.

For my finance and property LPA, my daughters have access to my accounts already through it, so that they can help me when and if I need them to, not only at a time when I lose capacity. Each bank will have their own separate system for registering this, and so it's worth checking with your own bank what documents they need to see from you to accept attorneys acting on your behalf. Of course, LPAs are not for everyone; not everyone has people they trust and who are willing to advocate on their behalf, for instance. This is why other forms of advance care planning are useful to ensure your voice is still heard in these important decisions.

It seems to me the system is unnecessarily complicated; it could be much simpler and help not only the patient but the doctor. It is not mandatory to have any advance care planning (ACP) in place and, as we've discussed, we're rarely prompted to do so. In fact, in a study published in *The Lancet* in January 2020,[1] of 6,072 patients presenting to hospital with an acute medical emergency, only 290 of them had an ACP. In patients less than eighty years old, only 2.9 per cent of people had one, compared with 9.5 per cent of people over eighty. I find it staggering how low those figures are when you consider how important this documentation is in terms of receiving the care that we want. It explains to me why whenever I write a blog about advance care planning, I have such a huge response. People are clearly curious about it, it is something they know they need, but the sheer complexity of it, navigating all the individual pieces of paperwork and different NHS trust systems puts people off. If only we had a system as simple as the organ donation one.

Clare explained it very well in terms of what we should be doing and at what different stages of our lives. She said those with chronic or life-limiting illnesses need an advance care plan, but those who believe themselves

[1] Thomas Knight et al., 'Advance care planning in patients referred to hospital for acute medical care: Results of a national day of care survey', eClinical Medicine, *The Lancet*, 19 January 2020, www.thelancet.com/journals/eclinm/article/PIIS 2589-5370(19)30240-8/fulltext

to be in good health should be advance care *planning*. Writing a will is, for example, part of advance care planning, and we should all have one of those, but according to one survey three in five UK adults do not have a will.[2] Understanding that we should all be advance care planning, no matter what our health status, was the lightbulb moment for me.

One of the forms that some people want to put in place is the DNACPR form, which stands for 'do not attempt cardiopulmonary resuscitation' – you can see why they've shortened it! It is also the one that we tend to hear of most often (surprising, considering that just one in five sick older patients in the UK have a 'do not resuscitate' order in place, according to a study published in the *British Medical Journal*,[3] despite the fact that many of these people are at high risk of cardiorespiratory arrest and that attempts to resuscitate them are likely to prove unsuccessful).

This piece of paper could form part of your advance care planning, but it is not legally binding; it is simply a tool to tell doctors, nurses or paramedics not to attempt to resuscitate you, even if your life depended on it.

---

[2] '31 million UK adults don't have a will in place', Canada Life, 25 September 2020, www.canadalife.co.uk/news/31-million-uk-adults-don-t-have-a-will-in-place/#:~:text=Three%20in%20five%20(59%25),not%20chosen%20when%20they%20die

[3] Jane Walker et al., 'Do not attempt cardiopulmonary resuscitation (DNACPR) decisions for older medical inpatients: a cohort study', *BMJ Supportive & Palliative Care*, spcare.bmj.com/content/early/2021/08/16/bmjspcare-2021-003084

Cardiopulmonary resuscitation, or CPR as we more commonly refer to it, can be made up of chest compressions, inflating the lungs and defibrillation (electric shocks to correct the heart's rhythm). We most often see depictions of CPR on TV and in movies, when a doctor will step forward with a defibrillator and order people to stand back and apply a shock to restart someone's heart. Often in these dramatic depictions, the heart restarts and all is well, but that isn't quite always the case. This type of resuscitation is usually only lifesaving in an otherwise fit and healthy person who suffers a sudden cardiac arrest; it is not a suitable treatment for 'ordinary dying'. There is a huge difference between a patient whose heart is the first organ to stop working (as in a cardiac arrest), and one whose heart is the last organ to stop working (as in the case of ordinary dying).

We met with Rebecca Langley, who was diagnosed with stage 3 bowel cancer when she was thirty, after living with ulcerative colitis throughout her twenties. Six weeks after major surgery, including surgery to create a stoma (where part of the bowel is brought to the surface of the abdomen so that waste can be collected in a bag), Rebecca started a course of chemotherapy, which resulted in an uncommon reaction followed by a series of four cardiac arrests, during which doctors performed CPR in the form of compressions on Rebecca's chest. While recovering in intensive care, she was told this intervention had fractured four ribs, but it was only months afterwards that doctors revealed this had also fractured her sternum and three vertebrae. The medics had saved her life but had inadvertently left her with many other injuries.

'You get different types of patient, don't you? And I wanted to know everything,' Rebecca said, 'but I think, had I not asked, I would have got hardly any information from doctors. I think they mentioned the ribs being broken in intensive care because obviously they had to check my lungs, but I didn't find out about the vertebrae for eighteen months. I'd been in back pain for all that time, and I think it was a rheumatology consultant who just dropped it into casual conversation.'

Because of the reaction Rebecca suffered as a result of the chemotherapy, the doctors are extremely reluctant to give her another course if her cancer returns, though for now the news is good and Rebecca is clear of cancer. After another recent surgery she is recovering and hoping to get back to full fitness again (despite her injuries, Rebecca completed a triathlon a year after her first surgery in 2018, and a half marathon sixteen months after her ICU stay).

'I'll probably have backache for the rest of my life,' she says. 'My ribs aren't too bad most of the time, but if I get exhausted then it feels like a horse has kicked me.'

But despite how well Rebecca has recovered from her cancer and the injuries caused by the CPR, at thirty-six she has a do not resuscitate order in place.

'You only ever see a glimpse of someone's life, don't you?' she says. 'Even in the last week I was in A & E again, so the me you are talking to now is very different to the me who couldn't have spoken to you then. After this call, I'll probably go back to bed. I haven't been abroad for twelve years because of my ill health. I have tried to hold down jobs, but it is impossible because of my exhaustion. I'm in pain and on bad days I can't look after myself. I'm certainly not financially independent and I live at home with my mum, and although I'm extremely grateful for that, I don't want to be living at home at thirty-six. My life isn't what I want, and you have to make the best of what you've got, but I certainly couldn't deal with a second recovery. The way I put it is it's not a wish to die, it's a wish to not suffer. There is no reason why I should have a cardiac arrest again, but I know that if I were to arrest, all my paperwork is in place. I would now refuse all chemotherapy, all surgery. A lot of people look at it as a negative, but for me it's not a negative – it's me taking control and saying I don't want to die, but I don't want to be trapped in this body that can't do what I want it to do.'

It seemed to me it was that word 'control' again; once people realise that they can take control, that they can question medics, they give themselves permission to disagree with them. But as Rebecca told me, they don't always like to be challenged.

'I always say to medics, "What would you do if it was your wife?"' Rebecca says. 'Because that catches them out. They say: "Oh, that's a bit personal," but I'm like this is my life, this is all I've got. And the other thing I struggle with is that they don't see the recovery. My surgeon knows I've had a rough time at home, but he doesn't know how much weight I've lost or how much pain I'm in, or how many times I've been in A & E, and he just goes from surgery to surgery to surgery.'

I could see how frustrating that would be to someone like Rebecca, though perhaps it is the same for me too: the consultant I saw when I was diagnosed, who had done their job and sent me away with a diagnosis, their file closed, didn't see all that I then had to live with.

I couldn't help feeling sorry for Rebecca, a young woman in her thirties whose life has been hijacked by hospitals and surgery and treatment. But here was a woman who is confident to question the medics. Going through paperwork has made me feel more in control, and that is important when you have a disease that has invaded your brain or your body.

'I don't see my wishes as a negative,' Rebecca said. 'Everybody should ask themselves: "Do I want to be resuscitated?" and it doesn't matter if you do or if you don't, but write it down and have the paperwork. For me it comes back to control. I've taken control. We plan everything else – our wedding, childbirth – why not this?'

As I said to Rebecca, it's the need to feel at peace, which completing the paperwork and talking brings.

Peter Hallgarten is five decades older than Rebecca but his own 'do not resuscitate' order and advance decision to refuse other life-sustaining treatments gave him peace of mind when he was admitted to hospital with Covid in 2020. I asked Peter whether he felt a certain calm with making peace with death.

'I think, when one feels one has had a long life and a good life and everything is in order, there comes a time that you can't fight something that's going to happen. You can fight to get well by mentally saying, "Well, if I go, I go, but on the other hand I'll try not to," but it was quite clear that I wanted no intervention. That was clear from the very start.'

Peter and his wife had registered their documents with the doctor ten years before, while in good health, and I asked him why they had felt the need to do that.

'I had been interested in "dying well" for about ten years when the subject was first raised in the patients' group of my GP surgery. Making an advance decision was logical and obviously sensible. Our confirming motivation was an aged friend who didn't have an advance decision. It was very upsetting – the in and out of hospital to keep this person alive who didn't want to be alive. The obvious thing was to make sure that one didn't go through the same process. I think it's actually good to do that because you don't want your family to see you in a really unhappy condition and being kept alive when you have chosen otherwise.'

Peter has decided that he chooses quality of life over quantity of life, and I can quite understand that.

Some areas in the country have what is called the ReSPECT form, which is a process initiated by clinicians and used to outline how you would and wouldn't like to be treated in the event that you do not have capacity to make or express a choice. What I was surprised to learn is that these ReSPECT forms are not legally binding; they are only a recommendation to medical staff, and they are intended to respect both patient preferences and clinical judgement. The ReSPECT form must stay with the person. I keep mine in my fridge at home. It might sound like an odd place, but the Lions Club International came up with Message in a Bottle (MIAB), which helps paramedics or other emergency services find your medical details and your next of kin if they attend you in your home. More than 6 million MIAB kits have been dispatched in the UK. I also have a sticker at my front door telling emergency services to look in my fridge for my own medicine and wishes. You can get these kits free from the Lions Club (lionsclubs.co/Public/messsage-in-a-bottle/).

It still seems so strange to me that there is not one centralised system and that all the various pieces of paperwork – some legally binding, some just recommendations – have to be done separately. But the more you have in place, the more likely you are to have your wishes carried out. It is also worth finding out from your GP whether there are other forms used by your own NHS trust because the closer you are to speaking the language of the medical staff that might attend you, the more chance you have of being cared for or treated in your preferred way.

Even though I had my own advance decision to refuse treatment, I still wasn't sure if I had done it correctly; for example, if there was a form I needed to sign, like the ReSPECT form, or if my ADRT was meant to be attached to some other document. Clare put my mind at rest by looking through it and confirming that, as with the other documents, there is no centralised system. The difference is that, unlike the ReSPECT form, the ADRT is a legal document, and so you have to be over the age of eighteen to write one. You must have the mental capacity to understand what you are writing, and it must include the statement: 'I refuse this treatment or treatments even if my life is shortened, or ended, as a result.' You must also have the form witnessed, and my suggestion would be that your GP would be a good person to help you do that, because they can also vouch for your cap- acity to sign the document, even though this is not a legal requirement. The charity Compassion in Dying has a very simple advance decision form which comes with guidance notes that the NHS links to. It was developed in collaboration with a range of individuals, medics and legal professionals and they have a free nurse-led help-line making the whole process easy.

It is worth pausing here for a brief word about doctors: I know how difficult it is these days to get an appointment to see a doctor, harder still to see the same doctor each time you visit the surgery. But my advice to those who are living with chronic or progressive conditions is to be patient and wait for an appointment to see the same doctor so you have consistency in care. This whole planning process, and the process once any illness advances, is much easier if your doctor knows you, has followed the trajectory of your condition, and has observed the consistency in your thoughts. It is worth putting the time in to establish that relationship, if it is possible.

There are many organisations that can help you write these documents, but the Compassion in Dying website (compassionindying.org.uk) has some great resources and templates and a free nurse-led help line that can make the job easier.

And so to the elements that make up your ADRT. It is worth quickly explaining the difference between an advance statement (a document detailing what matters to you, with all your likes and dislikes, and how and where you wish to be cared for that could be a good reference point for somebody caring for you in the future, particularly if you have lost capacity), and an advance decision – also known as ADRT (a document detailing treatments you may wish to refuse).

In your ADRT you have a right to refuse any treatment, which includes cardiopulmonary resuscitation, artificial ventilation (when you receive mechanical help to breathe), any treatments designed to replace bodily fluids, including blood, a pacemaker, feeding tube, antibiotics, chemotherapy and dialysis. What is important is that what matters to you is set out in a clear and specific way. An ADRT can be a very blunt instrument, and mine also includes the fact that under no circumstances do I want to be admitted to hospital, even if it would preserve my life (hospital admissions can be frightening, overwhelming and confusing for those of us living with dementia, and once you are in the system, it can be very difficult to leave it again). But there are other treatments that could be given that might be considered as comfort care. For example, those who lose the ability to swallow might need pain relief to be administered through a syringe pump or a PEG tube, and an operation to organise the latter would require surgery and a hospital admission, so the wording of each individual's ADRT must be specific. Every case scenario must be posed and thought through, and it must be written in language that medics can understand, as discussed earlier. That is why I believe they should be written with the help of a professional. It is also really important to remember that the ADRT becomes applicable once someone has lost the capacity to make their own decisions about that specific treatment.

My own ADRT is the blunt instrument I describe here. I have thought through every scenario and I am happy with what I have written down, but when going through my paperwork with Clare, it was her job to test me to make sure that I understood the importance – and any consequences – of what I had written down:

CLARE: Wendy, your first statement on your advance decision to refuse treatment says: 'When I am unable to communicate decisions about my medical treatment, I refuse all treatments which may prolong my life.'

WENDY: Yes.

CLARE: This is absolute, and it doesn't think about different situations. For example, if you were to go for a walk today and fell down by your duck pond and banged your head, would you wish treatments to bring you back to the Wendy you are today?

WENDY: If an opportunity comes for a way out then I will take it – Anna might not be very pleased if we haven't finished the book, but...

ALL: *laughs*

CLARE: So I am going to play devil's advocate here. You are campaigning, you are educating, you are bringing joy to your daughters, you are doing the things that make Wendy Wendy at the moment. Are you really sure this isn't enough for you, because if you have an accident and we could look after you with life-sustaining treatment for two weeks and bring you back to this Wendy, would you want to be this Wendy?

WENDY: No.

CLARE: Now that's a really clear no. From talking to you and from reading your books, I understand what you're saying, but for some people that's too much of a blunt instrument and someone else might say: 'Well, I hadn't thought of that.'

WENDY: This came up during Covid because I was talking with lots of my friends who have dementia and we were talking about if we got Covid and would we want all the treatment, and lots of them did, but I didn't.

ANNA: Wendy, can I ask you a question which I have been meaning to ask you for a while? I know that you have had antibiotics for a chest infection in the last year or two, so why did you have those antibiotics if you feel like that?

WENDY: Because I was still able to walk about, I was still able to do things. I wasn't knocked out and needed to go to hospital, but in the circumstances when I am unable to communicate that I don't want them, I wouldn't want them.

ANNA: Yes, but this is what Clare is saying to you, if you went to the duck pond today and you got knocked out, you could come to.

WENDY: But they don't know that, do they? They don't know that at the time that I am knocked out, and if an ambulance came and took me to hospital, then I don't want to go because I'm not able to communicate my wishes, and they don't know what state I'll wake up in; they don't know if it will affect my dementia being unconscious for so many days in hospital. Just being in hospital for a fortnight will affect my dementia, so I wouldn't come out as the Wendy I am now. That would be my opportunity to get out and I'd be quite happy to take it, whereas if you get a chest infection you just need antibiotics to make you function more easily.

CLARE: This is such a valuable discussion, and I understand what you're saying, Wendy, so if you took antibiotics for a chest infection in your own home, you would be making that decision. However, if those antibiotics didn't work and you needed intravenous antibiotics, which you could only be given in hospital, that would be your cut-off?

WENDY: Yes.

CLARE: So antibiotics in this case for Wendy are simply what I would call symptom control, because having a chest infection is horrible, but we'd be doing something that is non-invasive and that you remain in control of. We're not taking you to hospital and putting a line in your vein and giving you antibiotics.

WENDY: Yes, because a week in hospital for somebody with dementia is like a year in hospital for anyone else, and I wouldn't be willing to take that risk of coming out of hospital a week later and not knowing how I would be. Even when I fractured my wrist, I refused to be an inpatient to have the operation, so they did it as a day patient.

ANNA: But during the pandemic you had months of not being able to go out and so you forgot how to book a train ticket, for example, and when we were allowed out, you had to learn all that again, and you did it.

WENDY: Yes, but I could still do all the other things that were important to me – walking, even if it was only once a day, seeing my daughters, typing, taking my photographs. So if I forgot how to travel, it would be disappointing but it wouldn't have been one of the four things that gives me joy.

ANNA: Sorry to push you, but I find it really interesting to know where your lines are.

CLARE: I think this is exactly where we need to be, because people think an advance care plan to refuse treatment is simple, but it isn't. So I have a question for you, Wendy. You could require artificial fluids and hydration temporarily, so are you saying that you wouldn't want nutrition and hydration to bring you back to the Wendy you are now?

WENDY: If that meant being in hospital, no.

CLARE: So your cut-off is being in hospital rather than the treatment itself.

WENDY: Yes.

CLARE: So then we need to put that on your advance directive, that your bottom line is that you do not want to be admitted or taken to hospital.

Perhaps it sounds harsh to you, reading that conversation, but it was a helpful conversation for me. By having Clare and Anna probe me about my wording and various case scenarios, I was not only able to clarify to them where my boundaries lay, but also clarify in my own mind that under no circumstances do I want to be an inpatient in hospital, even if this led to my death. I know this is not a decision for everybody. Many people feel very safe in hospital, and I understand that too – after all, I spent much of my career working in one – but living alone and having dementia is not a good mix to have when faced with the possibility of being hospitalised; to be discharged would be a mission in itself. What have I got against being admitted to hospital? Particularly as my daughter is a nurse and I'd trust her with my life, but she knows me, and that's what it boils down to: she knows my wishes, she acts on my wishes. Hospital staff, no matter how compassionate or caring, simply won't know me and won't have the time to get to know me – particularly in an emergency. They might act in a way that does not leave *them* open to scrutiny about what care I receive, and that might not be in accord with *my* wishes. A hospital is the worst place for someone with dementia: our routine is gone, our familiar surroundings disappear and are replaced with a new and totally alien environment full of noise and people we don't know. I've had so many people tell me how they or their loved ones deteriorated with their dementia due to a hospital stay. There is no stimulation, no familiarity in hospital. I may leave mended physically, but my dementia would have declined to the point where I might not be able to return to living independently.

Clare admitted that she was surprised by the choices that I am willing to make, even ones that might shorten my life, and perhaps you are too. Clare looks at my life and sees it as fulfilling, vital – she looks at the valuable contribution I make by writing my blogs and this book that you hold in your hand, but that's just how we perceive other people, it's not about how people feel themselves.

At the end of the conversation, Clare said to me: 'It is my professional job to challenge you, and Anna has as well, and you've not once said: "Oh, I hadn't thought of that." You've said that would be your "get out of jail free" card. You've said: "This is a brilliant life and I'm living okay with dementia and I'm meeting the challenges; however, it isn't my choice to live like this." So this advance decision to refuse treatment really does say what you want, and you've thought about all the options that we could have put in there.'

It's true, it does say what I want, but at the same time I understood what Clare was saying to me, as so many people have been surprised by the hard line that I take, but then they don't see all the hours of my day that might not be so good and might not be so fulfilling, and yet I have to live them. Perhaps it is hard for those who are not living in ill health physically or mentally to fully grasp what life is like for those of us that are, and ironically, those are the people who are making the decisions about whether or not to allow us to have the ultimate control over living or dying – but we shall come to that.

If it was nerves I felt when awaiting my daughters to go through the decisions on the paperwork, they instantly disappeared on sight of my girls and instead, I was flooded with the usual love and happiness. We sat down with all the documents that Clare had checked for me and I took a deep breath and when I looked up at my two lovely grown daughters before me, I was suddenly taken back to a time of sitting them down as girls, of educating them about the world, of helping them navigate squabbles or things that had gone wrong at school, telling them of the importance of good manners, of working hard in their education. It has been a journey of lifelong learning that we have taken together, and yet why did I feel deep down that the decisions I had committed to these pages would allow me to take a first step on a path away from them?

It was their questions that snapped me back to the moment, the various scenarios that they posited to me, much like Clare and Anna had during our conversations, and yet although it felt quite different hearing these 'what ifs' from the two people I adore most in all the world, they weren't able to throw anything at me that I had not considered before. As I answered each scenario gently and confidently, I saw the understanding dawning in their eyes; all the grey areas they needed clarifying I was able to turn to black and white. I felt immense pride, relief and, yes, love, as they told me individually that they understood my wishes. It feels wrong to say they were happy with the part they would need to play in enacting them, if and when the time comes where they will be speaking on my behalf, but I think they felt more confident that they understood exactly what I was asking of them.

With that business out of the way, I pushed the two boxes towards them and watched their eyes light up as they pulled on the gold ribbon, and the cakes and pastries hidden away inside revealed themselves. The conversation turned to laughter as I realised they were both going away two days later, and they had so many treats to get through before then.

'Well, you've got enough for breakfast, lunch and dinner then,' I joked as they headed towards the door.

It was nice to end with laughter and yet why did I feel so alone – the house so silent – once they had gone?

Speaking to my girls was just one of the conversations I needed to have, the other was with my GP. I hope I have impressed on you in these pages the importance of sharing your thoughts, feelings and wishes with your doctor, the importance of that consistency of care because, after all, your GP may well be the gatekeeper to your future care, whatever your state of health now.

My own GP is used to my random requests and questions – in my last book I wrote about turning up at her office and sliding towards her a permission slip to enable me to do a skydive – only this time I went to see her, I had an altogether different piece of paperwork to share with her.

After working with Clare, my advance decision was similar but even tighter than it had been before to include the fact that under no circumstances would I wish to be admitted to hospital. I was braced for the 'what ifs' that my doctor might throw at me, just as I had been with the girls, and Clare and Anna, and I was ready with answers.

I had also added that I wished to die in a hospice and not in my own home. I know that many people ask to die at home, but I didn't want my house to be associated with death. I did not want Gemma and Stuart, who live in the village, to walk their dog and look up at the windows knowing that behind them was where I took my last breath. Staff at my local hospice, who I have got to know through the various talks I have done there over the last few years, have always assured me that they would be able to keep me comfortable, control any pain and the atmosphere would be much calmer, plus the bonus would be their beautiful garden, which I would be able to look out on to.

These changes would need to be solidified by the addition of my GP's signature on my ADRT, but I wasn't sure what her reaction would be to my request not to be admitted to hospital, and so I felt unusually defensive as I sat down in front of her and passed her the piece of paper. I watched as she read it, her eyes scanning the words, reaching the end and then starting again at the top of the page, although this time reading more slowly, taking it all in. There was a long silence between us while she did this and I searched her face for clues as to what she might be thinking, pre-empting any questions or challenges that might be forming in her head, readying myself with any answers.

She sat back finally. 'What if...' she began, and I smiled back.

'I bet you won't ask me anything I haven't already been asked,' I said.

I could see she was determined to try.

'What if you broke your leg out walking?' she asked.

I held up my wrist, reminding her how they put it back together again in day surgery when I broke it a couple of Christmases before.

Her shoulders relaxed, content that I had indeed been through every scenario. She paused, then leaned forward as she signed her name in ink.

'You know, Wendy, I knew all this already,' she said. 'I would never send you anywhere you didn't want to go.'

I looked back at her, into those kind eyes, I had no doubt that she meant it. But just in case, my ADRT is now uploaded to my file, and I left her surgery just that bit more assured that I have made my thoughts and wishes known.

# 4

## CONVERSATIONS ON
## ASSISTED DYING

It was towards the end of 2021, when my sudden weight loss became apparent. I'd been visiting my friend Philly, on the Isle of Lewis in the Outer Hebrides. The land-scape there is barren, rugged, the winds like no others I had experienced in my life and rated by Philly by how many pegs it would take to keep a piece of her washing on the line – this particular day, as we headed towards the sea cliffs behind the house to spot the seals, was a 'five-pegger'.

I shuffled behind with my camera, stopping every so often to peer through the viewfinder, amazed again at how the seals had appeared at the sound of our cries, marvelling at how close they felt, and pausing continu-ously to hitch up my trousers at the waist as I fought a losing battle with the gales. As a result, we didn't move quickly enough to avoid the incoming storm, so by the time we got back to the house we were soaked through, our hair seasoned with the salt carried on the wind, rain and sea spray, yet we laughed, invigorated, full of life as, again, I pulled at my trousers to keep them from slipping down towards my pelvis.

In the last few months I'd already shrunk from a size fourteen to a twelve, but now even that size hung off me and a size ten desperately needed a belt. It was when I was home that I mentioned it to my physio, Helen, as she pushed a steroid injection into my screaming hip at the GP's surgery the following week.

'It's probably all the walking I've been doing,' I told her, trying to take my mind off the length of the needle. 'I've lost a stone in the last month alone.'

I searched her face for clues in much the same way a passenger checks the faces of airline crew in turbulence. Because there was, at the back of my mind, my own nagging feeling.

'Have you mentioned it to Dr Clarke?' she said, keeping a poker face.

'No,' I said, 'but I've got an appointment with her next week, so I'll try to remember.'

'Write it in your book,' Helen said, as she jotted down my next appointment in biro in the notebook I take to all my medical appointments, a reminder to myself for the reason I'm there, the questions I need to ask, complete with spaces underneath for whoever I'm seeing to write the answers so I'll be able to tell my girls what they said when they ask.

The following week, I sat in the surgery waiting room trying not to feel too nervous. Not nervous because of the reason I was there but simply because I always fear that the GP will forget about me, or that she might call me and I won't hear, or that I might be sitting in the wrong waiting area. She's always running late, I told myself, fumbling in my pocket for the bright red note-book. I opened it and the words 'weight loss' stared back at me. I hadn't been over-worrying, just a slight niggle now and then. I'd mentioned it to the girls, but only because I was unsure whether to buy new trousers now or wait and see if I regained a few pounds. Not feeling hungry means it's easy for me to skip meals; it's why I set alarms in my iPad to remind me to eat, and the only reason I do that is so I have something to fuel my walks.

'Wendy?'

My GP appeared outside her door. I followed her into her room, the same familiar picture of horses on the wall, the window open, the light flooding in. We exchanged pleasantries and then finally I mentioned this sudden weight loss. Her face was calm, non-expressive.

'Do you know how much you used to weigh?' she asked.

'I remember getting to ten stone and being horrified,' I joked, trying to lighten the conversation because there it was again, a creeping, nagging feeling.

She walked me over to the scales and I held onto her arms so I didn't stumble as I stepped on. The needle jolted this way and that and then came to land.

'Hmmm, fifty-two kilos,' she said.

'What's that in old money?' I asked.

'Just over eight stone,' she replied. 'Let's do some blood tests.'

I sat patiently as she prepared some vials and another large needle to take some blood from my arm.

'Do you think it's cancer?' I said, as the hot, sticky liquid rushed from my vein into the plastic vessels.

She was used to my direct questions and replied that we'd need to rule out a few things and, yes, cancer was one of them. I let that sink in before I came out with what was really on my mind.

'You know if it's cancer I don't want treatment?' I said confidently.

My doctor had helped me fill out my ReSPECT form a year before, so she knew how strongly I felt on these matters, but I still felt the need to say it. I still needed her to know.

'Yes,' she said, 'but let's cross that bridge if we come to it. Come back and see me in two weeks and I'll have the test results by then.'

I spent that two weeks mulling over the idea of cancer in my head. I know that for some people it is their worst nightmare, and I don't want to belittle that or suggest

I don't understand what that fear looks like for them, but for me it started to represent something different – a release from dementia. It suddenly felt like the answer, a chance for my body to give out before dementia folds its fog around me. I asked myself over and over in those two weeks: was I sure that I didn't want treatment? And always the same answer returned to me: yes. I wondered whether to tell the girls, or wait for the doctor to confirm it. I had shrugged off their concern recently when Gemma had mentioned the weight loss, saying I just wasn't eating enough, but I knew I wasn't able to pull the wool over Sarah's eyes – she worked with cancer patients as a nurse. I wondered if she was already seeing me as one of them.

On bad days, when my head was thick with fog and the headache rapped at the inside of my skull, I told myself again that cancer would be the perfect way out for me, my escape route from the later stages of dementia. In those moments, self-pity evaporated and it felt like a blessing, which I knew few people would understand.

I started embracing it then, playing with my thoughts, making plans: how I would tell my daughters that I didn't want treatment; talking through palliative care with my doctor; how I would explain to other people that I didn't want treatment – no, that would wait; my life, my choice; I didn't need to explain anything. I would become the lady with cancer, not the lady with dementia.

I have always coped in life by turning negative news into a positive, and this experience was no different. Two weeks on from my blood test, I was back in Dr Clarke's peaceful little room. This time I felt more relaxed, hopeful even. I told myself that pain relief was so much more advanced these days, that I'd never have to suffer like Mum and Dad. I could live my life to the full knowing that the end was coming. From hereon in it would be quality, not quantity of days – I felt quite calm at that thought.

Once more, my GP helped me onto the scales. The needle righted itself at forty-nine kilos.

'That's a drop of three kilograms in a fortnight,' she said. 'You have been eating, haven't you, Wendy?'

'Yes,' I promised her.

She went through all the test results. Her face was one of concern, confusion, as each of them was in the normal range.

'So what is going on?' I asked, though more out of curiosity than fear.

Despite the blood tests coming back negative, I was convinced cancer was still lurking inside my body somewhere.

My doctors arranged for scans and ultrasounds of my chest and stomach, which I duly attended, and ten days afterwards, as I stood in line at the surgery for my Covid booster, I spotted my GP coming out of her office with a huge smile on her face.

'It's good news,' she said, taking me into her office. 'All the tests came back negative, no cancer detected.'

She paused, waiting for me to mirror her relief and joy, but inside my mind had to do a quick unscrambling of all the thoughts that had preoccupied me for the last few weeks as the door to my escape route slammed shut.

'Oh, that's wonderful, isn't it?' I said flatly, more for her than me.

'I'll explain fully next week at your appointment,' she said, and with that, she was ready to call in her next patient.

I left the surgery feeling sadness instead of the happiness I knew I should have felt. I felt guilty – of course I did – for all those people who would do anything to walk out of their health practice with good news like that, for all those who have to deal with the reality of the opposite news and what that entails. So why did it feel like I had won the lottery and yet lost the ticket?

When I next saw Helen the physio, she was happy too that it was simply all the walking I was doing that was the reason for my dramatic weight loss. I played along, but I was desperate to say to somebody – anybody: 'But that was my legitimate way out of dementia.'

Instead, I just smiled. For them, not me.

If only the medical system offered me an escape route, though; if only those of us who are tired – so tired – could choose instead to rest finally. Not all of us with chronic, progressive or terminal illnesses, but those of us who would prefer to avoid the later stages, those of us who would like to plan the end of life like we have planned every other part of our lives, those of us who would like to say goodbye while we still can, those of us who would like the right to consider assisted dying.

If only.

So often this book has come back to one word: choice. We've looked at how people want to die, what is important to them at the end of life: being surrounded by family and friends; not being in pain; being in their own home. And we've looked at talking about decision-making in terms of treatment: what treatment might be wanted, if any, or how people might wish to be treated if they were hit by a bus tomorrow and could no longer speak for themselves.

Choice. It is at the centre of everything we do as humans every day – or at least those of us lucky enough to enjoy the choice of bodily autonomy, and who are not bound by regimes or other strict diktats. And yet, we have no choice over when we die, or at least we don't in the country I live in.

I rarely meet people who know exactly what I'm talking about, and how having that choice removed affects us, but I also know I'm not the only person who thinks about the end of life, what that might look like and how much control we have when it comes to how it happens. I asked my friends living with dementia if they have similar thoughts, and I was surprised at just how much it plays on people's minds:

GEORGE: Because of the various diseases I've got and the fact I have such a lot of painful, tired days, I frankly think about myself more than I should and therefore I tend to think about death isolated from anything else, or anyone else. I do think about when I might feel the time has come to maybe eat some foxglove, or something, or hemlock. I honestly do. In fact, I was having a conversation with my support group this morning and I dropped in a little bit about foxglove and suicide and whether it would be a gentle slipping away or not. And one guy said: 'Gordon Bennett, you're usually quite positive,' and I said: 'I'm not negative, it's just there will come a time when I want to think seriously about this.' I had three days – Sunday, Monday, Tuesday – when I felt lousy and I was foggy and I was faint and I'm in pain from my feet, and I thought: *Oh God, I hope this doesn't last long, because*

*I don't want to be alive if it's like this*, and one day it will come to that, and I would quite like to be able to dig up a foxglove, make a potion and get rid of myself just when I choose, but on the other hand, I'm not sure I ever will. It's such a difficult thing to pin down. We don't want to, do we? Who wants to pin down that they're going to take their own life? You've got to have a very strong commitment to a humanist end of everything, and I have, but I still enjoy things.

WENDY: I think that's the key thing you said there, George, 'I hope it doesn't go on long.' It's when it does, day after day after day, that those thoughts start to creep into your head, because it's rubbish and still enjoying things isn't possible on those days.

GEORGE: Exactly, and as long as I can get enjoyment reasonably frequently... on a day like today – okay I'm tired at times, but I'm feeling reasonably good – I just get enjoyment watching the clouds go over and the trees in the wind and everything else, because I'm not thinking about pain. I don't know how people who get seriously into cancer cope. Maybe there's always that thought that they're going to get through it.

WENDY: And also their brain isn't affected. Our difference is our brain is affected, not some other organ that's invisible. The disease is going on inside and causing you pain maybe, but your head is able to function. It's the days when my head isn't able to function that I start to hope it doesn't go on for many days, because it's the continual fuzz that's difficult to cope with.

GEORGE: It's like looking through tissue paper all the time, or cotton wool. You just can't quite get out of it and you can't see things clearly, you can't think clearly.

WENDY: And those with cancer may take an extra dose of morphine to get rid of the pain, but we have no escape from our symptoms.

GAIL: On those days, you just want to come back, so you try everything possible to bring you out, like going for a walk or taking a photo, hoping it will lift the fog. And the pain in your head – it's not like a headache, I don't know what it is; it's just there, and it stops you from thinking and finding your words. It's annoying.

WENDY: And two paracetamol doesn't make it better. When I said I've got a banging head, it took a while for my daughters to get that: 'Have you taken something?' No, because it's not that sort of pain that's treatable with tablets.

GEORGE: It's almost a metaphorical pain. Dementia reduces your ability to process, to understand what your senses are telling you, so sensory overload becomes very uncomfortable very quickly, and for me, it's that overload of pain and fatigue that overwhelms me sometimes, and if that comes along at the same time as I'm having a tired, foggy day, what do you do about that? There's nothing you can do, but the trouble is thinking about suicide. It's one of those days when you might think: *Shit, I've had enough of this.* We're used to having days like that, but not too many of them at once, and if you do have a few together, that's when you really start to get down and look into your soul and almost say: 'What the hell is the point?' And what happens when we, with our failing brains, are unable to actually think about tomorrow being okay?

WENDY: I totally agree. In my mind, it is just that; you're in the fog and I can think at this moment, *Hopefully tomorrow will be a better day*, but when I don't have that ability to think tomorrow will be a better day, to me that's when I'll have gone over the edge.

GEORGE: Yes, you have to be able to recall the good days in order to be aware that they're possible again.

WENDY: For me it's the intuitiveness that we have at the moment. It's when that goes, when I'm no longer intuitive, it's the dementia that's causing me to feel like that, because I've floated over the edge into permanently being unable to analyse what's going on in my head.

GAIL: Will we actually know, though?

WENDY: Well, that's the million-dollar question.

This is the side that we rarely show other people, not even those who are close to us – perhaps *especially* not those who are close to us – and this is why support groups for any condition or illness are so vital, because they allow us to talk about these innermost feelings. If we can talk about them, they don't overwhelm us, they lose their power over us.

## A CONVERSATION WITH SOMEONE LIVING WITH MS

Sometimes when people talk about ending their life, it is just a manifestation of the helplessness they're feeling, just a way of expressing in words how hopeless they feel. We're all allowed to feel like that from time to time. What is important is being able to talk about it, to wander down that path – perhaps with someone's hand in yours – and then to wander back, choosing life for another day. Talking and planning for end-of-life care is not the same as having suicidal thoughts. Mostly, to talk about death is to choose life, until you feel you can no longer make that choice. But when do you stop choosing life? That is a really interesting discussion.

Anna introduced me to her best friend, Jane. Jane is British but has lived in the United States for more than twenty years. After the birth of her daughter, Emily, who is now twenty-two, Jane was diagnosed with multiple sclerosis. She went on to have her son Elliot, now twenty, but two years ago her diagnosis was changed to one of secondary progressive MS (a type that worsens, with no periods of remission). Last year, Jane was fitted with a baclofen pump, which delivers medication directly to the fluid around her spinal cord, and which has reduced the spasticity in her legs, but in doing that has left her paraplegic and Jane now uses a wheelchair. Her condition also means that she suffers from bowel and bladder incontinence, neuropathy (a painful condition when the nerves in the body's extremities are damaged), and the absolute fatigue that MS brings to those who live with it. Jane lives in Minnesota with her partner, Tavis, who cares for her alongside his own full-time job.

Jane is a very special person to Anna. I know from our conversations just how amazed Anna is by the way her best friend copes with her own progressive illness and how proud she is of her.

It is often left to those who are healthy in body and mind to make laws which govern us and how we live or die. We can take control within the realms of these laws, and putting together my advance care plan definitely made me feel more empowered, more in control, but for me there still remains a grey area, a sense and worry that perhaps my wishes would not be taken into account in the event of an emergency by paramedics, who need to act fast lest they face scrutiny for not doing something in the course of their duties. I understand as well that it goes against a medic's values to appear not to help somebody, but for some of us that's exactly what we're asking for. Some of us are waiting for that 'get out of jail free' card, a chance to be released from whatever disease has burrowed its way inside of us, squatting in our bodies and changing our lives.

Perhaps these types of feelings can only be truly understood by those who are living with these conditions – people like Jane.

Jane agreed to talk to me about that dilemma of when to stop choosing life, and in particular the importance of personal choice.

I started our conversation by discussing with her the fact that we are reminded by the government, by medical professionals, our whole lives to take responsibility for our health, yet when it reaches the final stages of our lives they snatch that responsibility away by not letting us take control of the way we die. Jane agreed.

'It's like all the technological advances that have been made in medicine are always about keeping someone alive as long as possible, and not everyone wants that. Society is so focused on that – it's like you're a rebel if you say: "No, I'm good, thanks."'

The way that science has forged ahead with medicine is keeping people alive for far longer. One woman I know with cancer feels obliged to stay alive because the medics have been keeping her alive. The family of another friend of mine were never asked when she was in intensive care if they wanted to stop treatment, so the family assumed: 'Well, she must be saved, then.' But her quality of life is so poor now; she doesn't go out any more; the only place she goes is for dialysis at the hospital, and that's not a life she would have chosen, but she's been forced into that life by the decisions the medics made for her. It's not something I would ever want to happen to me.

Jane agreed. 'I'm very clear about it. I joke about getting a tattoo that says "do not resuscitate". Because we have the "do not resuscitate" forms in America, and I'm sure you have them in England, but my worry is, if I have a car accident or something, are they going to check my file before they commence any kind of resuscitation? Because if I was sitting in the passenger seat, they wouldn't be able to tell what was wrong with me, I would just look like anyone else. I don't want them to make a mistake because I've made it very, very clear, that living like I live right now, I'm right on the edge of not wanting to be here. I spend a lot of my time thinking about that and processing it and thinking, *Can I continue and for how long?* and so I'm very clear that if I were in an accident, I do not want them to bring me back, and if they were to, I would be so pissed off.'

I loved Jane's idea of getting a tattoo. We even joked about having 'please turn over' in brackets on our backs – though I did threaten to put 'do not resuscitate – or else!' Only, trying to find a tattooist who would agree to 'ink' me proved impossible and that made me really sad.

Jane and I are total opposites: she has a fully functioning brain and it's her body that lets her down due to her MS, and I have a (sort of) fully functioning body and it's my brain that lets me down, and I don't know which is worse. In reality, neither is worse and shouldn't really be compared, but when I think about the things that make my life worth living – my own personal dealbreakers – they tend to be physical: going for long walks; taking photographs; typing; and, of course, my two daughters. But for Jane, she is in a situation where she can't walk, and so we couldn't possibly consider the same things.

'Since I started using a wheelchair in 2021, I've seen myself become really depressed and stay in bed for days at a time because I just didn't want to go on,' Jane told me. 'And then something shifted. I worked with a physio and now I'm able to get in and out of bed on my own. I practised and I adapted and now I'm able to use the bathroom on my own, so we adapt, right? I was thinking about what my dealbreaker is – and it's a tough one to say out loud, because I know there are people with MS who live like it, so it makes me nervous to say it's my dealbreaker – but as far as I'm aware for myself, it would be losing my arms and my hands, because that's what I use to transfer myself, and also needing a catheter and having to self-catheterise.'

As humans we adapt to whatever is thrown at us, but Jane would need to assess her quality of life if she lost the use of her arms. The first thing I thought about was that she would not be able to hug her children if she lost the use of her arms, but that's because I do not have to think, day to day, of the practicalities of moving myself. The matter of quality of life is so individual; it always comes back to choice.

'The adapting thing is really interesting because, you just adapt, right?' said Jane. 'Like how you set alarms on your iPad, but my question is when do we get to that point where we've done enough adapting? I would like to get to a point when it's okay for me to sit down with the people I love and say: "Okay, guys, I'm done adapting. Like, I know I could keep adapting, but I don't want to adapt any more, so can you give me your blessing and can we all just be okay with the fact that my level of adaption stops here."'

It was so true what Jane said. It comes down to her level of adapting – or indeed mine, or anyone else's reading this book, because we are the ones who have to live inside our own individual bodies and minds. There are people really happy with a life, no matter how hard it is. They want that life, they're willing to keep adapting just to be able to breathe air, to bear witness to life, and I respect that. But like Jane, I know that I will eventually reach my limit in terms of how much adapting I am willing to do, and how much it exhausts me to do that each day, how much the balance will tip between quality of days and quantity. Why doesn't society accept that we have a right to choose what that quality means to us? The only thing we have no choice in whatsoever is when we are born, but everything else should come down to personal choice, and that includes death. It doesn't seem right that it's still frowned upon or illegal for us to choose when we've had enough, particularly when we've exhausted all the support there is out there for us. And it is actually because of that lack of choice at the end, because of what the current law imposes on us, that many people end their lives sooner than they'd wish, or alone.

## THE LAW AS IT STANDS

Perhaps here is a good moment to pause and look at what the situation is in this country and beyond with regards to assisted dying. There is currently no legislation in

England and Wales that allows for assisted dying. Taking your own life is legal, but under the Suicide Act 1961 it is currently a criminal offence to help someone to take their own life. This is punishable by up to fourteen years in prison. A YouGov poll in 2021[1] found that while 73 per cent of people in the UK thought assisted dying should be legalised for the terminally ill (which still would not help me), just 35 per cent of MPs agreed. The issue not being a priority for our current Members of Parliament means there is little chance of a change in law any time soon – certainly not in my lifetime.

Baroness Meacher's Assisted Dying Bill, which would allow a terminally ill patient to take prescribed life-ending drugs, provided they have the consent of two medical practitioners and the High Court, passed a second reading unopposed in the House of Lords in 2021. According to the bill, this would apply to terminally ill people with capacity to make the decision who would be 'reasonably expected to die within six months'. A witnessed declaration would need to be approved and countersigned by two independent medical practitioners. Those doctors would need to examine the patient and their medical records to be satisfied that they were terminally ill and that their decision had been reached voluntarily and on an informed basis

---

[1] Euthanasia, YouGov, yougov.co.uk/topics/politics/explore/issue/Euthanasia?
content=surveys

without coercion or duress. All of that sounds reasonable to me, but opponents of it argued that doctors sometimes get prognoses wrong. They asked: How could the doctors be sure that someone had less than six months to live? How could they be sure that someone was not acting under duress? They also asserted that this might open up the vulnerable to family members intent on profiting financially from their premature death (even though it could be reasonably expected that those same people would be dead within a few weeks or months in any case), and anyway, the bill failed to make progress before the end of Parliament that year, and so no law was introduced. No subsequent bill has yet been introduced in Westminster, though the Health and Social Care Select Committee did launch the first ever House of Commons inquiry into assisted dying in 2022, the outcome of which is expected in 2023.

A petition by Dignity in Dying's Sarah Wootton reached over 100,000 signatures in June 2022 and so secured a Westminster Hall debate among MPs in the House of Commons, the first time assisted dying had been debated there in over two years.

Scotland might be able to move forward on this issue within the next few years, though. A public consultation on assisted dying in 2021 had an unprecedented response totalling almost 15,000 people, and three quarters of respondents supported the proposals in the bill, which also seeks to allow those with less than six months to live the chance to end their lives at their choosing. A final proposal for the bill has now been lodged at the Scottish Parliament.

In 2022, Members of the House of Keys voted overwhelmingly to give permission to bring forward assisted dying legislation to the Isle of Man, which is being drafted as I am writing. The States Assembly in Jersey has also voted in favour of a proposition to support a change in the law and draft legislation is being prepared, which may be implemented in 2024 or 2025.

The British Medical Association (BMA) dropped its official opposition to a change in the law on assisted dying in favour of neutrality on the matter during its Annual Representative Meeting in 2021. Likewise, the Royal College of Physicians, the Royal Society of Medicine, the Royal College of Nursing, the Royal College of Psychiatrists and the Royal Pharmaceutical Society all now hold neutral positions.

Medical assistance in dying has been legal in Canada since 2016, and in Colombia, and the US, assisted dying is now an option for terminally ill, mentally competent adults in their final months of life in eleven jurisdictions: first Oregon in 1997, and since then Washington, Vermont, Montana, the District of Columbia, California, Colorado, Hawaii, New Jersey, Maine and New Mexico. Following a public referendum in 2021, New Zealand legalised assisted dying for terminally ill citizens, and legislation has been passed in all states in Australia.

In Europe, Spain passed a law allowing assisted dying in 2021. Assisted dying became legal for Austrian citizens who are terminally ill or have a permanent, debilitating condition in 2022. Switzerland, Belgium and Luxembourg all have right-to-die laws in place.

In the Netherlands euthanasia and assisted suicide have been legal since 2002 for those who are experiencing 'unbearable suffering with no prospect of improvement', and people can make an advance directive to receive euthanasia even after they have lost capacity, as would be the case for dementia patients. This law was tested in 2016 when a Dutch doctor was taken to court for administering a fatal dose to a patient with Alzheimer's. While she still had capacity, the patient had made an advance decision for her life to be ended before entering a care home, adding that she wanted to decide 'while still in my senses and when I think the time is right'. The doctor, along with two other doctors, decided to act on her previously recorded wishes, but when the day came to end her life, a sedative was put in her coffee and she lost consciousness, only to wake up again. Her daughter and her husband had to hold her down while the fatal dose was administered by the doctor. Prosecutors believed the woman had showed resistance to her previously stated decision, though the woman's daughter felt 'the doctor freed my mother from the mental prison which she ended up in'. The doctor's decision to act was upheld by the Supreme Court in 2020, which believed she had acted in accordance with the patient's wishes.[2]

The advance decision this patient had made before she lost capacity meant that she had a safety net; it also meant that while she still had capacity, she could review the directive regularly and amend it where necessary. Most importantly, she could get on with living in the knowledge that, when the time came, someone would help her die in accordance with her own wishes.

There are days, and often weeks now, when the light fails to cut through the foggy days that descend on me. On those days there is no sunshine to burn away the clouds. In those moments I cannot make sense of anything around me. I might as well be inside a black void, untethered, an abyss. Times like that might last for minutes, hours or days. The longest time recently was a week, and the only thing that kept me going was the thought that tomorrow might be better. I comforted myself that if that hope was still able to cut through – if I could still rationally think tomorrow might be better – then I wasn't there yet, I hadn't reached that edge. But where is the edge? Is it still somewhere ahead of me in the fog? Is it after

[2] Daniel Boffey, 'Dutch doctor acquitted in landmark euthanasia case', *Guardian*, 11 September 2019, www.theguardian.com/world/2019/sep/11/dutch-court-clears-doctor-in-landmark-euthanasia-trial

the next step I take, or the next ten? It is impossible to know, but once I go over it, I will be deemed to have lost capacity. I won't be able to make decisions for myself any more, my power of attorney will kick in and my daughters will speak for me. I feel the urgency now to express my wishes, yet no law will support my decision to end my life before dementia claims me completely.

In this country, we are still so far from making assisted dying legal for the terminally ill with less than six months to live that the thought of the British government implementing a model similar to the one in the Netherlands feels impossible. The Dutch model would allow me to assess how the last six months of my life had been, it would give me control over whether I felt those foggy days were coming more frequently, it would release me if I felt the edge was within my next footstep, and most importantly – and this is the bit people forget – it would allow me to focus on living while I still could.

## CONVERSATIONS WITH A PALLIATIVE
## CARE DOCTOR

But even if the law was changed tomorrow, even if the choice were open to me to choose *how* I die, to choose *when* I die, how might I know that the time was right?

We discovered in the last section that there are many things in place already in law that allow us to have more control than I actually thought; however, for me a lot of those things would kick in once I have already gone over the edge. But I am still adamant that I don't want to go over that edge. For me, if I lost the ability to take photographs, I could do without the camera because I could look at photos on my iPad, so the three things that are left are: a) if I didn't recognise my daughters, that would be the first and worst thing; b) if I could no longer type because that's my escape from dementia; and c) if I could no longer walk, that's my final happiness gone. But those things could well happen in the latter stages, my body might fail after my brain does, and then it would be too late to make any decisions. This is my conundrum. Some of my friends would say they plan to be in a nursing home and they haven't thought through going over the edge because they're happy with whatever happens, but for me, I'm not happy with being that person, dependent on care. I might be happy when I'm there, but I don't actually want to be that person. That's the dilemma. I wanted to talk to Kathryn Mannix about this.

'It's a massive philosophical question,' Kathryn said, 'because you're completely right, there may be a Wendy that can't walk on mountains any more, but who can sit and watch videos of people cycling over the top of Striding Edge, and who loves and is fascinated by watching that, and knows that she loves being in the mountains but can't quite remember why.

You can make a decision as this Wendy – the one you are today – that prevents that Wendy from having that experience because she would die in advance because you would have refused a feeding tube, for example. But then you're in the philosophical dilemma of: "But what happens if that Wendy is happy watching her videos and looking at her photos and only pottering short distances?" And we can't know that without time travel, and that's the dilemma isn't it?'

I'm so clear in my head that that isn't the person that I want to become, so right now I am confident in thinking that although I might be happy, or I might *seem* happy, I don't want to be that person. Kathryn seemed to understand this.

'I absolutely hear you, Wendy, and what I'm thinking of as you're saying this is my lovely father-in-law, who died, and seeing him in his residential care home, so diminished from the outdoor person, the bird watcher, the bow-and-arrow-making-for-his-grandchildren man that he had been, and it made me very, very sad, and yet he relished every instant cup of coffee, even though he'd been a real coffee connoisseur; he relished chatting to the guys in the home about trivia that wouldn't really have interested him when he had his full intellect. Yes, he was always a little bit perplexed about why he wasn't coming home with us. He was not unhappy but, equally, he was not him.'

When Jane and I had our conversation, she put it in a nut-shell for me when she said, 'There'll come a time when we've had enough of adapting.' I wouldn't be waving that white flag to dementia then, I'd instead be saying: I'm done with you and your games, no longer am I going to risk the chance of you winning.

And that brings me back to the last thing Kathryn said about her father-in-law: he was not unhappy, but equally he was not him. Kathryn mentioned the things that surprised her that he was able to enjoy. What she didn't mention was the rest of his existence. Could he dress himself? Take care of his personal needs? Or was he reliant on the care of others? For me that reliance is a non-starter. The Wendy as I am, the independent Wendy who still lives alone with dementia, who, yes, has her daughters, her community, Alexa even for com-pany, works hard to live an independent life. What does it matter to me if I have several pairs of the same colour trousers to slip into each day? At least it means I can still put them on because I am familiar with the routine of fastening them. I have the same tops in various different colours, but what does that matter if it means I can remember how to dress myself each day? Thinking of a time when reliance on others becomes more personal – intimate, even – is simply not on my agenda, and don't I have a right to decide that? I have to stress again, I've no fear of dementia, or even death itself, what I'm saying is that for me personally, death is a better option than living as a person who is totally reliant on others and bears no resemblance to the person I am now.

## A CONVERSATION WITH AN ADVOCATE FOR ASSISTED DYING

Nobody could fail to be moved by Paul Blomfield's emotional speech in Westminster Hall the last time assisted dying was debated by Parliament in 2022. Paul is the Labour MP for Sheffield Central, and he has used his own personal – and heart-wrenching – experience to attempt to persuade his colleagues of the case for assisted dying. Paul's father was eighty-seven when he died alone in the garage of his home in 2011. He had been diagnosed with terminal lung cancer and chose to end his life prematurely to avoid the last few weeks and months with the disease. He did not tell his family or his partner of his plans for fear of making them complicit in his decision, and it is the loneliness of Paul's father's last moments that causes his son so much distress, even years on.

'I still find it difficult to talk about even privately, I think that was obvious in the discussion we had in Parliament,' Paul told us when we met. During the Westminster Hall debate he was, quite understandably, hardly able to control his emotions recalling his father's story, but he agreed to meet with me to tell me more.

'So if we unravel to before my dad was ill, he'd had a good life and at eighty-seven he'd seen a lot of friends go, and he'd often seen them go in circumstances that were distressing and he could see no purpose in those deaths for his friends, or himself. So he'd been through all the issues about choice at the end before he'd had to face up to them, and he was clear that we ought to have that right to die, which he obviously then exercised when he was in that position, but as I said in Westminster Hall recently, it was still a shock to me because he had a terminal diagnosis but he still had quality of life.'

I could see from what Paul said that his dad felt similar to how I feel: that he shouldn't have to make a decision prematurely, and if the laws were more flexible in this country, he wouldn't have had to.

I found it so brave to hear Paul standing up in Parliament and sharing his father's story, but, as he says, it's important to bring real-life experiences to Parliament, whatever the subject.

'The tragedy of my father's death was not that he died; he had a good life well into his eighties. The tragedy was the *way* in which he was forced to do it, making what I describe as a lonely decision but also a very lonely death. I think too often this debate focuses on people's fear of changing the law and what I've tried to focus on is that we should recognise what the *existing* law does to people. I'm absolutely convinced that if the law was different, my father would have lived longer, which contradicts one of the arguments that opponents to assisted dying put forward: that people would be encouraged by a change in the law to take their lives early. It is the *current* law that encourages people to take their lives early, because people act when they know they still can because they're frightened about losing control. Another argument opponents make is that everything would be fine if there was a wonderful palliative care system and obviously there should be and that's absolutely right, but our palliative care isn't good enough, and my father took the decision to end his life shortly after he had met the Macmillan nurse, who had talked about his pathway through his last few weeks, and I think that helped to crystallise his decision, because I think it's this fear of losing control.'

For me Paul hit the nail on the head when he said it's not about changing the law, it's facing what the current law does – it actually *prolongs* death, and not life. The public are always reticent to make big decisions to change the law, but these circumstances exist for people like Paul's father, or me, because governments *won't* make those big decisions. And there lies the tragedy. So many people exist who feel just like Paul's father did, or I do, and we're not saying – and I'll just use dementia as a case in point – that everybody in the late stages of dementia should have assisted dying, because that's just wrong, but the choice we haven't got at the moment is whether we accept that existence in the late stages, and I believe that should be our choice. Paul agreed with me.

'I think that's at the heart of the argument,' he said. 'It's about people *choosing* the quality of their life and choosing the right moment when they feel there is insufficient quality in their life. I've listened carefully to the arguments on both sides and some of the people making the arguments against assisted dying in Parliament are my friends whom I agree with on many other issues, but I think there is a disingenuousness there. Many people are hiding behind arguments about palliative care, or hiding behind arguments about the pressure that it would put on people to take their lives prematurely, and behind most of the arguments against assisted dying is people's personal faith and the belief in the absolute sanctity of life, and my point to them is: "If that is your view, you live your life by it, but don't force others to do that."'

Paul did give me some positive news, though – he feels that minds are changing, slowly but surely. He told me that in the most recent Westminster debate there were two or three of his colleagues who said: 'I used to be against a change in the law but now I support it.'

'I think the balance is changing in Parliament,' Paul said. 'I'm not sure that we're quite there yet, but the view is changing in the medical profession, in other jurisdictions; in other countries we're seeing legislation, so for me it's only a question of time before we change the law in England and Wales. But my concern is how many more people have to have the distressing death that my father faced by the time we change the law.'

It comes back to this argument again, there is a 100 per cent certainty that we're going to die, yet so little emphasis is put on having a good death. But it takes people to be in a situation like ours to see the simplicity of it. I am not saying that people *need* to have my view, I'm saying that I should have a choice to have my view and they should have a choice to have theirs, and if they don't want to take advantage of those laws, then don't, but let the people who want to, do it.

Paul's story was so heartbreaking in its detail – little things like how his father had organised his affairs in the moments before he ended his life, leaving piles of cash to pay his bills. I can see how upsetting it was to Paul that his father did those things alone, that he had no one to share those burdens with, and that he wasn't able to put his affairs in order with the support of his family.

I feel like that with dementia, that I need to choose to die while I still can. Likewise for those with more physical disabilities: they must choose to go while they still have the ability to carry out the physical act: to take the lethal dose, as in some American states, or administer the lethal injection into their cannula, or take their lives in other ways too desperate or dangerous to write about here.

In the Netherlands, they have a phrase for needing to go before life gets untenable: they call it 'five to midnight'. When I learned this, I was minded to use it as the title for this book. It has a Cinderella quality to me, the sense that you need to leave the party just before everyone else. Everyone else is going to leave too, you just need to leave sooner to prevent real suffering.

Hiding behind the argument that we need to have a better palliative care system instead of giving people the right to die is just not good enough. I have already written that our focus must and should be on palliative care for a whole host of reasons, not least because we read in one report that the figures will skyrocket in the future, simply because modern medicine is keeping so many more people alive with complex care needs. But palliative care has never been a focus in the NHS since its creation; it has been more often the remit of charities, and we need to let go of the idea that if we kick assisted dying into the long grass, we will instead live in a utopia where our palliative care system is perfect.

As Paul said: 'We have to recognise that even the very best palliative care doesn't mean that everybody can die in that Hollywood image of gently passing into the night without pain or upset. I've known many people in palliative care who have died awful deaths and those who are running those facilities have done their very best, but some diseases are very cruel and beyond the capacity of palliative care to provide that ideal ending that is the implication of those who argue that's the alternative.'

## A CONVERSATION WITH AN OPPONENT TO ASSISTED DYING

I have noticed during my conversations with people that it is palliative care staff who have the most resistance to legalising assisted dying, which is strange when you think that they are the people who have seen death, and per- haps suffering, up close more often than the rest of us. A 2020 survey by the British Medical Association found that while 40 per cent of doctors supported a change in the law that would see physician-assisted suicide, 70 per cent of palliative care doctors opposed it and just 7 per cent showed support for it.[3] I can't help but wonder if the increasingly litigious world we live in has some bearing on this opposition among palliative care doctors – the responsibility they would feel and the possibility of facing a lawsuit, like the doctor in the Netherlands.

Anna and I met with Baroness Ilora Finlay of Llandaff, a palliative care professor who sits in the House of Lords. She is a vocal opponent of assisted dying, and we

[3] *BMA Survey on Physician-Assisted Dying*, 2020, www.bma.org.uk/media/3367/bma-physician-assisted-dying-survey-report-oct-2020.pdf

were curious to hear her reasoning, particularly as she had worked in that field for her entire career. Baroness Finlay, like many opponents, believes that palliative care can and should be able to provide comfort to the dying.

I started off by talking to Baroness Finlay about how we like to think that we can offer the right care so that people won't feel that their lives are intolerable, and acknowledging her concerns that if we allow assisted dying to be made legal, there wouldn't be the emphasis on care that there should be, but I also wanted to tell her, firstly, that I think we have to be realistic about the type of care that is on offer currently, and secondly, how some people don't want to have to keep adapting to have their needs met, and surely that is their choice?

Baroness Finlay replied, admitting that people were not getting the care they needed, but then went on to talk not about people who are living with progressive or chronic illnesses, but overworked NHS staff.

'The frontline staff are exhausted,' she told me, 'and if you look at the people who are looking after patients who are dying, they do not want to be giving them lethal drugs, they do not want to be in a position of judging who is eligible and who is not eligible.'

I re-emphasised my point, saying that of course we need to change society, of course we need to fund the NHS better, but in the meantime there are people – like me – who choose to want to die rather than adapt to the poor system and poor care we have at the moment. But Baroness Finlay again wanted to focus on a broken system. I didn't feel like she was hearing what I was saying.

'Let me just stick with the system at the moment,' she said. 'Don't forget that the NHS was founded on the principle of a community looking after its own, and I don't think we're asking it to change; I think we're asking it to reclaim its fundamental values. Now you talk about adapting – we all go through life with life events and we have to adapt to life events all the time – the mother whose child dies will feel overwhelming grief, for example, the people who I have met in the greatest despair were the parents of a child that was murdered, and they could never forgive themselves for having let their child get into the situation where the child was murdered, and they had to live with that for ever. I think that must be, I would say, impossible to adapt to. We all know of particularly young women, but some young men, when a relationship breaks up they feel totally hopeless; we know of young people who have severe depression, for them they see no future and yet later on, as they adapt, they have a life…'

It seemed to me that Baroness Finlay had a very specific idea of what can be tolerated, and what can't be. But she couldn't seem to see that, for someone like me, the adapting might become intolerable, as intolerable perhaps as the lives of those parents she mentioned. She described my pleas to consider assisted dying as wanting 'death on request'. But that is oversimplifying a complex argument way too much. I reiterated to her that my wish isn't for when I'm in despair: it's my wish because I don't want to live in the end stages of dementia.

Baroness Finlay asked me what I was most frightened of.

'I'm not frightened of anything,' I told her. 'The Wendy that I am now believes that I wouldn't want to take that chance of being the Wendy that I may be in the future – of not knowing my daughters, not being able to walk, not being able to go outside in the countryside, not doing the things that are important to me.'

'At what point do you want to be given lethal drugs, and who is going to decide that for you?' Baroness Finlay asked me.

'In the current situation it would be me deciding before I go over the edge

'How would you know when you go over the edge?'

'Well, you don't, and that's the problem. You have to choose death sooner than you need to simply because you need to have the capacity to make the decision.'

What Baroness Finlay seemed to be concerned about was protecting medics from having to make decisions about ending someone's life and she considered a system where doctors aid dying as 'diverting resources away from providing care into assessing whether now is the time to end someone's life'.

We challenged her, saying that doctors do that every day in the course of their working life; she pushed back again, saying that doctors look at something like cancer and decide what the treatment is, and what are the benefits and the risks. But the word 'benefit' to me sounds very subjective. Something one doctor might consider a benefit, might be very different from what another doctor might say. And so I believe I am right when I suggested to her that doctors are making these life-and-death decisions every day.

'No, not really, because if you know the stage of disease, the histology, the type of disturbance, and you know what's available – for example, forty years ago eighty-five per cent of children with leukaemia died, now eighty-five per cent of them survive. The treatment is difficult, yes, the treatment is punishing—'

But again, I needed to remind her that we were talking about people with terminal progressive illnesses, and still she insisted that children's leukaemia was once a terminal illness.

The conversation felt very frustrating, Anna stepped in to try to explain to Baroness Finlay, as I was having a particularly foggy day.

'I understand that medical treatment has advanced,' Anna told her, 'but we are talking about a situation where somebody has less than six months to live, or a progressive illness which is not going to get better. There is no chance – it is only going to get worse and their life is only going to become more intolerable or more painful.'

But again, Baroness Finlay was preoccupied by the decision over who was going to decide for someone like me, who may have lost capacity to make that decision.

'Who then decides today is the day to give her lethal drugs? And why are you wanting to put that as part of her medical care, and not leave it completely outside and independently assessed?'

We posited to Baroness Finlay that she was more focused on protecting medics in their working lives, and asked her how protective she feels of the patient who is living with a terminal illness they find intolerable.

Baroness Finlay denied she was protective of doctors, but then did quote anecdotally cases of medics she had heard of in Canada who were leaving their profession because they didn't want to be giving lethal injections. She also spoke about the emotional and psychological toll that it takes on doctors, carrying out medically aided dying. Baroness Finlay insisted it was important to listen to patients, but it didn't feel that she was listening to me. I asked her what the alternative was to not having these decisions made by the medical community.

'We used to hang people for crime,' Baroness Finlay said. 'Why did we stop hanging people? We stopped hanging people because sometimes innocent people were hanged. There were mistakes. The balance is what is the risk? Is the risk on one side greater than the risk on the other? I would prefer that we veer on the side of supporting people to live rather than risking ending life when it didn't need to be ended. I have seen too many people where the diagnosis was wrong, where everything that could be done had not been tried, they had not been offered everything that was possible, or there had been unacceptable delays in offering, and I think that risk is too great. It's a balance of risks. I also think that it would be quite tempting, actually, to get used to ending life. I always remember one Dutch doctor who had said the first time was really difficult, the second time was easier, and the third time it was a piece of cake. Now I find that worrying – killing somebody should never be easy.'

Anna reminded Baroness Finlay that she had commented on the importance of listening to patients, and asked her again to listen to me.

'I feel like the care system for those with dementia is down to a postcode lottery in terms of what sort of care you get,' I tried again, 'but regardless of that, even if it was the best care I could possibly get, I still don't want to be that person who has lost the things I value now, regardless of how miraculously the care system is reinvented to be.'

Baroness Finlay asked me to cast my mind back to my twenties.

'Are the things that you value now the same as the things that you valued then?'

'No, of course not,' I said.

'So you have adapted and changed,' she replied.

'Yes, but in my situation, it won't be an adaption for the me that I am now, it will be an adaption that's brought on by other people because I'll no longer be totally capable of making those decisions for myself.'

'You are talking from your standpoint. I am not passing judgement in any way on you or your thinking – where I am coming from is I am saying is it safe to change the law or are more people endangered if we change the law than if we keep it as it is? We have a population of sixty million in the UK, and in amongst that population there will be hundreds of people who think like you, and there will be hundreds of people who are endangered if we change the law.'

But what Baroness Finlay did not seem to be accepting was that those who do not want to choose assisted dying do not need to, but why deny those who do the opportunity to end their suffering? But Baroness Finlay was very focused on worst-case scenarios, people who might be being coerced into ending their lives, such as those living in poverty, or unable to speak for themselves.

'I can't ignore the fact that one in six elderly people are abused and it's behind closed doors and it's within their own families and not detected by a healthcare system,' Baroness Finlay told me. 'I have had so many patients who have spoken about wanting euthanasia, they wanted to go to Dignitas, then after they have said: "I'm really glad you could not give me lethal drugs."'

But it's the very fact that I won't be able to say those words in all likelihood – I won't be able to express that opinion – I'll be in the hands of other people to interpret my silence almost in a way that they choose. I agree with Baroness Finlay's concerns for those who do not have an advocate, but I was asking her to hear what those of us who want to make the choice now are saying. Those other people that she is worried about can stay within the care system to be looked after, as the law dictates they must be. I always advocate that people with dementia are just as important as anyone else, what I'm saying is I want the choice and other people want the choice to make that decision themselves while they're able.

'I think I am looking at this from the point of view of legislation changing, I'm looking at it from the point of view of safety of the population, of safety for the most vulnerable, and I'm looking at it from the point of view of how it can be abused. And you are looking at it from the point of you – Wendy today – and you – Wendy as I think that next month, the month after, the year after might be. And you see a future with no hope in it, and I want to have a future for people where we still find hope even if it's hard work, even if we have to search and we accept that everybody is going to die, some sooner than others, and people often die when they just let go of life. I've been with so many people and they just almost said goodbye to me and they died the next day of whatever their underlying condition was—'

We interrupted her to remind her that those people still have an underlying condition. Because to talk about 'killing people' is to use language that is simplistic and really quite frightening, and the people that the Baroness is talking about who simply 'let go' still had a progressive or terminal illness.

'But by the time you get to my age, we've all got underlying conditions,' Baroness Finlay insisted.

Again, it didn't feel like she was listening.

'The choice you are advocating is a very black-and-white choice; you are saying you're either alive or you are dead,' the Baroness insisted.

But that was absolutely not what we were saying, nor did we say that safeguarding and care systems were not important, but what we were saying was that when people have exhausted all those systems – the psychiatric, care, home pain management – there isn't anything more black and white than saying there is nothing you can do: you will need to just wait until you die.

'I can't say there is nothing more I can do,' Baroness Finlay said. 'I don't have a magic wand. What I can do might be very small, it might appear sometimes trivial, but if it brings comfort, it's worth doing, but I, as a doctor, and other doctors in my own discipline don't want to be in a position of saying: "Yes, you are eligible for lethal drugs – here you are."'

But what I didn't understand, and what I put to Baroness Finlay is that these people are already dying, their diagnosis alone would make them eligible, and their desire to end their life prematurely would see them seek to use any new law, while those who didn't want to wouldn't, so it wouldn't be doctors making a decision, it would be the patient – perhaps me. But this is something that Baroness Finlay could not seem to hear and I found that disappointing.

This was actually the second time we had met with Baroness Finlay online, and during our first conversation, she had impressed on us the story of a man she had observed in a dementia care home who played the piano pitch-perfectly for the residents every day, despite the fact he had advanced dementia. She wanted us to realise that his life still had purpose, not only for him in those moments he played, but for the residents, some of whom would get up and dance. This story stuck with me, not least because Baroness Finlay gave us other examples, other people who had pockets of moments that made life worthwhile, like, for example, the woman who was unconscious for days as she lay dying, yet roused herself long enough to tell her daughter, who had been keeping a bedside vigil, that she loved her before she took her last breath. These stories are, of course, emotional to hear, but I couldn't help but ask myself whether these tiny pockets of time made the rest of those people's lives tolerable. For example, what about the rest of the day that the man in the care home wasn't playing piano – how did he spend his time, was it locked in confusion or agitation? Perhaps he was perfectly content – it is quite possible – but it seemed to me that those on the outside looking in were deciding what made an individual life meaningful, and I wondered if that person were able to communicate, would he agree?

I have spent the last six years as I write this advocating that those living with dementia can lead meaningful lives and still contribute to society, but I have also said that when I tiptoe over that edge into a person who has little awareness of my surroundings, my loved ones, my sense of self that I have strived so hard to hold on to, life will cease to hold meaning for me. Should I not be able to make decisions for that me of the future?

## A CONVERSATION WITH A FAMILY MEMBER

Baroness Finlay, with all her decades in palliative care, seems to believe that it is possible to make someone comfortable right up until their last moments, but there are stories that suggest otherwise. Sarah Drummond's mother, Heather Black, begged her daughters to end her life when she was dying of oesophageal cancer. Since Heather's death, Sarah and her sisters have shared their story in the hope of changing hearts and minds – and laws.

Sarah admits that until her mother's illness, assisted dying wasn't really on her radar. She says that she had experienced many types of death in her family and describes them as having been 'manageable though not pleasant'. She says her mum's death was different; it was '*so* traumatic that we vowed when we stood in that room if we could stop even one person having to suffer in that way, we would'.

Sarah lives in Scotland, where some progress has been made with a proposal for draft legislation in the pipeline. If that law succeeds, it would have saved Sarah's mum from suffering in her last few days, but it wouldn't help someone like me. As Sarah said to me when we met, we have to accept that we need to inch towards change.

'With Mum, when we found out that there was nothing that could be done, that that was it, it was stage four, it was terminal, it was kind of damage limitation,' Sarah explained. 'It was the end of life and that's what we were facing at that time, so the Scottish Parliament bill would fit perfectly into my mum's situation. Obviously there's other people it doesn't, but to get any chance of getting it through, those parameters have had to be so narrow, so focused, so tight, because otherwise it's never going to happen, and that is the frustrating part.'

We have to go in these stages to get people used to the idea. Medicine has come so far that we can treat almost anything, so why can't we treat death? I read a quote from Sarah somewhere which said that that there is medicine in the world that could have made her mum's death easy, so she asked who she was being kept alive for.

'It makes no sense at all,' Sarah said. 'Mum spoke to us and she spoke to the person at the hospice and she said: "I've had enough," and if we had been lucky enough, we could have said goodbye instead of the trauma that followed, because the end actually made it worse, and rather than it being a nice, calm death, it was just horrific. Mum had this huge tumour that was wrapped around her oesophagus and she was making these choking noises – it sounded like she was choking to death – and they gave her some medication, which meant that she literally coughed and spat and gurgled little brown volcanoes for the last twelve hours. Bits of skin and blood and tumour just came out of her mouth – it was like something out of a horror film.'

Descriptions like these are hard to read, but not often talked about. What I find devastating for Sarah and her family is that these images, which are so unpalatable for many of us that we can't bear to have the conversations on assisted dying, will haunt her for ever. It means Heather's daughters had no closure to her death.

'We couldn't even say goodbye because we just went from one horrific event to another,' Sarah told us. 'It just doesn't make any sense: what benefit was it to anyone for my mum to be kept alive over that time? I know everyone says you wouldn't let animals suffer, but it's true, you wouldn't, and the other thing is, even if you're not suffering, it's up to you if you want to end your life.'

I've said throughout this section that we respect those who don't want assisted dying as a choice, that's *their* choice, but I believe others should be able to have their choice, people like Sarah's mum, who should have been able to say: 'I've had enough.'

'For us, the first thing we said was, "This is crazy – how can this be normal?" My mum was lying there, she was still alive – who is she being kept alive for? Why are we in this room? What quality of any kind of life is there left? For us it was what could we do to stop this happening to other people? And for ourselves: I wouldn't want my husband or my kids to go through that. More than once Mum begged us to kill her, *begged* us to end it, and we thought what can we do? We thought about it, about putting a pillow over her head, all those thoughts go through your head, but had we known where it was going to go, we would have taken matters into our own hands.'

It was so sad to hear Sarah's story, particularly the desperation she felt when her mum begged her and her sisters to help her die. It took me back all those years to my father's own cancer diagnosis, how the first thing he asked doctors was whether there was anything they could do so he wouldn't have that prolonged death, because that is what it is. We talk so often about prolonging life, but we are actually prolonging *death* by not discussing the suffering part of it.

Sarah admitted to me that the details of her mother's last few days are really unpleasant to hear, but she said: 'Not enough people tell those stories and after we shared our story, people wrote to us and said: "Oh, that happened to my granddad," or "That happened to my dad," but all this stuff is hidden in this lovely little idea of holding someone's hand as they die and it's just not the reality all the time, it's not the truth, and we need to talk about that.'

So again, we just don't talk enough about death. A lot of emphasis in the assisted dying debate is put on the safeguards that would need to be put into place. The topic is approached from a worst-case scenario stand-point, which, in my opinion, overcomplicates matters, especially when you think how other countries have managed to negotiate safeguarding.

Of course safeguarding needs to be in place, but in the case of Sarah's mum, no doctor could be in doubt that she wanted to be spared her suffering, no doctor could fear that she was making a decision to die because she was being unduly influenced by her relatives, no doctor could believe that she was choosing death rather than being a burden to her family, because there is no family in the world who would want to see their loved one suffer like that. As Sarah said, if they knew what had been in store for their mother, they may have made a decision to help her, even if that meant they faced prosecution themselves. As Henry Marsh said in his excellent book *And Finally: Mattters of Life and Death*, ending your own life is not illegal in the UK, yet it is illegal to help someone do that non-illegal thing.

## A CONVERSATION WITH A DOCTOR WHO ASSISTS DYING

During our conversation with Baroness Finlay, she spoke a lot about how doctors felt uncomfortable helping someone to end their life, though every assisted-dying law the world over has a conscientious-objection clause, so that no doctor would have to carry out an act they felt uncomfortable with, or that was against their individual principles. She described anecdotally how many doctors in countries that allow assisted dying have raised concerns about being compelled by law to help the terminally ill to die. It felt important to speak to a doctor

who does prescribe life-ending medicine to terminally
ill patients, to find out if it really did become, as Baroness
Finlay describes it, 'a piece of cake'.

In June 2016, the California End of Life Option Act
was written into legislation, meaning that terminally ill
adults living in that state were able to request a drug
from their physician that would end his or her life. To
be eligible to ask for 'medical aid in dying' (MAID, as
it is called in the States), people must be over eighteen,
have a terminal illness that cannot be cured or reversed,
have less than six months to live, have the physical ability
to take and ingest the drug, have the mental capacity
to make decisions, and not have impaired judgement
due to a mental disorder. There are many safeguarding
steps that are taken in the course of getting access to this
lethal drug including: the fact that patients must make
three requests to their doctor, one in writing; they must
see the doctor alone to make sure the decision is vol-
untary; they must see a consulting physician to confirm
their diagnosis is terminal; and the doctor prescribing
the drug must discuss other end-of-life options with the
patient and their family. A 2021 data report published
by the California Department of Public Health[4] showed
that since the law came into effect, prescriptions had

---

[4] *California End of Life Option Act 2020 Data Report*, July 2021, www.cdph.ca.gov/Progr
ams/CHSI/CDPH%20Document%20Library/CDPH_End_of_Life%20_Option_
Act_Report_2021_FINAL.pdf

been written for 3,766 people and 2,422 of those had died from ingesting the drug; the rest had not been used. This is consistent across the other ten American jurisdictions that have also legalised medical aid in dying, where around a third of prescriptions are not used.

Catherine Forest is one such doctor who writes these prescriptions for her patients. Anna and I met Dr Forest on Zoom when she was in her home in Santa Cruz. I started by asking her what she would say to people who describe doctors who prescribe lethal drugs as 'killing people'.

'When people ask me what I am doing when I'm prescribing aid in dying medications,' Dr Forest said, 'I say that I'm fulfilling my medical promise to them, which is to end suffering, as they define it for themselves, and I believe that it is the agency of the patient to tell me what their suffering is. I remind them that it is legal where I live and were it not legal, I would not do it, but I fought hard for it to be legal because I believe dying people should be able to make their own choices about the timing and the manner of their death.'

Dr Forest also has very personal experience of medical aid in dying. Her husband chose to use California's MAID laws to end his life in 2021 after he was diagnosed with an ALS-type condition (ALS, or amyotrophic lateral sclerosis, is what we more commonly refer to in the UK as motor neuron disease) thought to be Covid-related.

I was curious to ask Dr Forest what she thought the impact was on people living in a state that has legalised aid in dying, particularly because we know that a third of prescriptions written for lethal drugs are not used.

'I think that people knowing that they have the option of aid in dying live the life that they have with less anxiety and they're able to be more present with the people they love,' she said. 'I don't quantify that. I don't think I can translate that into more days lived, but I do think it's not quantity but the quality of their lives that is dramatically different and that's universal, actually, and that's whether someone chooses aid in dying or not. I hear all the time: "I don't think I'd choose aid in dying" – and they never even request it – "but I know that I could." It is a huge weight off people's minds. But as my husband said: "The drive to live is tremendous."'

As the law stands in California, at the patient's own request and if they meet the eligibility criteria, Dr Forest can prescribe somebody with a terminal diagnosis a lethal drink or a syringe containing a lethal drug that they administer themselves. The fact that patients must be able to administer the drug themselves means that some people who wish to take advantage of aid in dying are unable to because of the types of progressive illness they have – for example, those with multiple sclerosis or ALS, who may be unable in the later stages of their disease to physically lift and ingest the lethal drug. However, technology has been created that allows people to have the drug delivered through tubes or catheters, even at the command of the blink of an eye – the point is, it is still controlled by the patient. But the law still excludes somebody with dementia, who is deemed as not having the capacity to make the decision to end their life.

'In my jurisdiction, you have to have capacity at the time that you are dying,' Dr Forest explains, 'so, for instance, someone with dementia cannot access our law, which is a limitation of the law. I believe that it is possible for people to have a say in what they want in the future and their intentions for the future. That, in fact, is what a durable power of attorney for healthcare is in our jurisdiction. It says: "If I can't make decisions for myself, this person makes decisions for me." It's an intention for your future self that no longer has capacity for medical decision-making. However, in California there are no plans to widen the eligibility criteria, due to the complexity of the safeguarding required.'

It is strange that you are able – even in the UK – to refuse lifesaving treatment in an advance decision, outlined in the last chapter, in the event of you losing capacity, though that would be reactive to some other medical emergency or other medical condition occurring, but under Californian law someone like me cannot make a decision to end the suffering of my future self once I go over the edge. Dr Forest pointed out that in Canada the assisted dying laws account for people with dementia (whose deaths are deemed reasonably foreseeable), who are able to submit a waiver of final consent, so that their medical assistance in dying can go ahead even after they have lost capacity. However, crucially, they would have needed to pick a date for that to take place sometime in the future, and if they objected on the day 'by words, sounds or gestures', it would be invalid. Since medical assistance in dying was written into Canadian law in 2016 – and amendments were made in 2021 that widened the definition of who is eligible to include those whose deaths were 'not reasonably foreseeable' – 31,664 people in total have died using medical aid in dying.[5] The Canadian system would work for me, and I wanted to talk to Dr Forest more about this issue of capacity and future planning.

'I'm now a widow of someone who's used aid in dying, and my husband would have chosen to live longer, but because of our law, where you have to have physical capacity, he died sooner than he would have chosen,' she told me. 'So when I think specifically about dementia, one of the things you said, Wendy, is the ability to think: "I'm a human being with consistency throughout my lifetime; you know me, and I'm writing these things for you in the future who, as I am losing agency, can help me in

[5] *Third annual report on Medical Assistance in Dying in Canada 2021*, Government of Canada, July 2022, www.canada.ca/en/health-canada/services/medical-assistance-dying/annual-report-2021.html

this part of my life, the ending, this sunset. There is none of us who will not die, so is there a way for me to grant my agency to someone else? I know it's not going to be perfect, but if these conditions are met, can I shorten the period of time where right now I'm experiencing the knowledge I'll live that way as suffering?"'

Dr Forest admitted that she has treated a lot of patients in the end stages of dementia, people like me, who believed that they would be suffering once they have gone over the edge, as I say. But she said although to her they did not appear to be suffering, she knew as their family physician what they would want, and she would do 'the very best that she could do' by perhaps not transferring them to hospital to be treated for a bladder infection, to stop unwanted treatment and just take care of someone's physical pain.

'I can see exactly why we fight for inclusion rather than exclusion – because that's what it is currently: exclusion for access to agency at the end of life,' Dr Forest said.

I explained to her how the only option currently for me in the UK is to travel to Switzerland to end my life at Dignitas, but that I wouldn't want to die in a land that I don't know, and couldn't bear the thought of my daughters coming with me and then travelling back alone.

'We've all been living this for twenty-five years in the US, where you can drive to where it's legal and set up residency, but then you're not where you were a resident,' Dr Forest said. 'But the thing is, what is right for your jurisdiction? Has your society evolved to where they support it? I'll go out and talk to other physicians, and when we poll people, they support the option for aid in dying. It's when you get down in the weeds that you find out where people are uncomfortable, where society has moved or not moved, and around the issue of capacity, it turns out that's where some of the discomfort lies. Jurisdictions matter, so there is something similar between where you are and where I am that the concept of dementia means not being able to make a conscious in-the-moment decision, and that is in a lot of people's way. I have a hard time, because to me I should be able to say for the future, "I am clear now."'

I talked with Dr Forest about the advance directives available in countries like Canada and the Netherlands, where people can state their wishes before they lose capacity and then revisit them as the disease advances. In my case, dementia is fluid; if I'm having a foggy day, I wouldn't bank on me having capacity to do anything or say anything, whereas the next day, if the fog has cleared, I have full capacity again. So it's fluid for me even now, and as the disease progresses it becomes more fluid, I believe. But it's almost like dementia is too complicated for people to include in anything.

'I can see how it feels that way and it does to me too, to some extent. I do believe that probably the best way to think about it is that there really is a course to pretty much all dementias, where there's a beginning and a middle, and I believe that the next step is going to be that somewhere in the beginning and the middle, when it's clear to those surrounding that person that there's some consistency to their decision-making around what they imagine they would want at the end of life. In that case you would document that, and it will be a gift to their families and to their friends, because then there'll be some conditions about what advanced dementia looks like, and has the person arrived at it, and in those moments, all of the decisions, that agency, has been handed to the family medical decision-making – or who-ever has it – and one of the options will be aid in dying. In those options, one of them will be: you've known this person, have they arrived there? Is it time? And, as I said, there are no plans to change the current law, and it is a lot to ask a family member.

'You're saying it's a lot to ask of someone to come back without you from Switzerland, but it's a lot of respon-sibility when someone appears to be happy. You've been around dementia: people do not appear to be suffering when they're in dementia, so it's a lot to ask of another human to take responsibility for ending someone's life who does not appear to be suffering. So you have to tell them in advance: "This is my perspective now, looking at the end of my life in dementia; this is what suffering looks like to me, now trust me – trust me – do what I am asking of you, it will be a gift to me." And that's the complicated piece. I believe we will get there when we put in the context of all the options and in the early stage find the language for our future agency to say, "This is what suffering feels like to me, please do this." That's where I believe we'll go.'

Unlike Baroness Finlay, Dr Forest seemed to understand what I was saying about not wishing to go over the edge. The way she posited it to me when I explained to her was: 'You're not living the life your past self would want to live.' And that is exactly it, and it felt so refreshing to hear someone from the medical community acknowledge and respect that feeling.

'When people say suffering, it should mean "what does suffering mean to you?"' Dr Forest said. 'So for my husband, in his mind to have a feeding tube and a breathing tube was unimaginable to him, to not be able to communicate. He lived his whole life communicating. But I've had another patient who, as long as their mind was there, they were living. So this is why what you're saying is really important; you cannot denigrate another person's experience – you really have to listen. Who is Wendy? Wendy is saying the essence of Wendy doesn't want that future, and I know I will not be able to state it in the future, so I'm stating it now for the future. Trust me, believe me.'

I cannot explain the relief I felt speaking to Catherine Forest, someone who spoke my language but, more importantly, listened. To say she had passion for the topic was an understatement, but she also had compassion. She felt my frustration, she shared it; when she mentioned the word 'suffering' on many occasions, she listened when I explained to her that it wasn't future suffering I was afraid of but future living, that the Wendy now does not want to be the future Wendy, to have a life of reliance on others, no matter how 'happy' I appear, or, more accurately, no matter how people choose to interpret my facial expressions. Dr Forest could see the difference between someone in pain and suffering and someone simply not having the life they wish for themselves, just like her own husband had chosen, yet he had been able to act on it because of where he lived in the world.

I am forever being told by people – and its usually those who oppose assisted dying – 'but you might be happy', and I want to shout back at them: 'That's of no consequence to me!' To have no autonomy, no independence, to be totally reliant on others for when and where and how I do things, is not the life today's Wendy wants for future Wendy. Dr Forest was perhaps one of the first medical professionals I have ever spoken to who got this completely, who granted me the personal autonomy to state this, who believed me when I said it, who listened. How much we take for granted that simple act of listening, even listening without empathising, of simply saying to someone: 'I hear you, and I can see why you feel like that.'

As Dr Forest told us, it is when you 'get down in the weeds' that you understand what people's resistance is to changing the law and allowing people to have personal autonomy over their lives – all parts of their lives – but other jurisdictions have proved that this problem is not insurmountable; they have found ways around the safeguarding issues. But of course it remains complex. In Canada a possible extension to the law to allow those with severe and incurable mental illnesses like depression to be able to ask to end their lives is being considered (though it has been delayed until 2024 to enable legislators to further examine evidence and safeguards), and yet in England and Wales we still can't take the first step of not prolonging death for those with less than six months to live.

The whole conversation with Dr Forest was fascinating, and I wish I could write it all here, but what she also revealed is how she and other physicians can offer a legal alternative to those for whom the existing aid-in-dying laws do not apply. Dr Forest said that she offers support to patients both within California and outside the state who wish to voluntarily stop eating and drinking, known as VSED (often pronounced *vee-said*).

'I have people that I consult that have cancer and they're going to die within six months but they live in a state where there is no aid in dying, so what we do in those situations is after they have made the decision to voluntarily stop eating and drinking, we sedate people so they don't experience hunger, so they're sleeping until their organs fail and they die. This takes anything from seven to fourteen days. But the reason this is not [assisted dying] is because the thing that kills them is not my medications for sedation. What kills them is not eating and drinking, and they chose that – they are doing that to themselves. And in our jurisdictions, if you have the capacity, you have the ability to refuse treatment, including food and drink.'

Dr Forest pointed out that the sedation they receive is not terminal sedation: the patient is waking up and going back to sleep. She is simply managing their symptoms as they die.

'We've a number of patients over the years that had the diagnosis of dementia. They lived through a great deal of their dementia and then when they realised where they were heading, they shortened their lives sooner than they might have chosen just because they had the capacity still to voluntarily stop eating and drinking, and if they had waited longer, they would not. And that's sad to me, for the same reason as travelling to Switzerland, because they wouldn't necessarily have made that decision themselves; they felt like they were sacrificing quality days for capacity, and that's a trade-off. It's a shame that there's not the ability to have the life that you want in the time that you have.'

Those seemed the exact right words to me: the life that you want in the time that you have.

## A CONVERSATION WITH MYSELF

I wanted to look more closely at this idea of voluntarily stopping eating and drinking. I already need to set alarms on my iPad to remind me to eat and drink, so could this be a way of shortening my life so I don't have to go over the edge into a dementia where I am no longer able to care for myself? It would mean, of course, as Dr Forest said, that I would still need to go before I was 'ready', while I still have capacity to choose. This is the fault of those who make the laws – or in the case of this country, refuse to make them. Perhaps it feels difficult to read here that I might be seriously considering ending my life prematurely, but I need to be clear that having rational thoughts like this, having a curiosity with regard to options and dignity at the end of life, is not the same as having 'suicidal thoughts'.

I had never considered whether my own GP might be able to give me the type of aid that Dr Forest describes, care to keep me comfortable and pain-free if I were to choose VSED, and I was keen to know where the law stood in this country. Compassion in Dying offered to help me learn more. The national charity supports people to prepare for the end of life, how to talk about it, plan for it, and record their wishes with reference to the Mental Capacity Act 2005.

I met with Sarah Malik, clinical lead and services manager for Compassion in Dying, who told me that the charity receives frequent calls from people asking for more information about voluntarily stopping eating and drinking as a means to hasten their death. She explained that because there is currently – as I write – no clear, nationally recognised information available to the public or to clinicians in the UK, the care and support that patients choosing VSED can expect from their GP or other caregivers can vary widely. This is why in 2022, Compassion in Dying called for national guidance on VSED.

'We've got common law in England and Wales that says VSED is a legal option,' explained Sarah. 'But, crucially, only an adult with capacity can choose this, so it's not something you can add to an advance decision as these documents are only followed when you've lost capacity to make decisions about treatment. It's a choice that adults can make when they've got capacity and are usually also very unwell. I typically receive calls from people who are in the advanced stages of an illness – for example, cancer – and are concerned about having a difficult or prolonged end-of-life experience and wish to hasten it by stopping eating and drinking. But we've become acutely aware there is no clinical guidance.'

The Mental Capacity Act in England and Wales does not assume that someone with dementia automatically lacks decision-making capacity, recognising that it may fluctuate and that 'someone can lack capacity to make some decisions, but still have the capacity to make other decisions'.

But there is one catch, and it can be a big catch for people who have decided to see through the process to end their life this way – access to symptom management is not always consistently available.

Sarah explained that, 'saying no to food and water isn't saying no to all care – and it is certainly not saying no to pain relief and symptom management. However, without clear clinical guidance it can be difficult for your healthcare team to provide you with the most appropriate care that takes into account the choice you have made.'

Sarah explained that, if people do not want to take pain relief orally (because they would need to take tablets with water), doctors can assist them by prescribing sub-lingual tablets that just dissolve under the tongue, so there is no need to drink water. She described this as a 'supportive approach' – although not all settings tell patients that this type of pain relief is available.

The VSED process typically takes between seven and fourteen days, and the symptoms people tend to experience, such as agitation, can be similar to those which typically occur as part of the ordinary process of dying. Sarah recognises that it takes a certain type of person to have the determination to choose to die in this way, but for some, fasting is a very natural part of the dying process. In some cultures or religions this is a widely accepted and practised choice.

'You have to go into this process as planned and as transparently as possible with your clinical team; you really need them to support your choice and help you manage your symptoms. I would add it's also very important to have the support of your health and welfare attorneys, your support structure, who can help ensure your wishes are heard and respected. Another big part of my work is helping attorneys to be listened to. It's so important that attorneys understand their role and responsibilities and use your written documents to keep on top of things. Your attorneys or carers should work with the clinical team to agree how to support the fast and how to manage symptoms, for example, by ensuring that big trays of food are not brought in and that dry mouth and agitation are properly managed.

So where does the law stand on this matter in England and Wales? Father-of-two Tony Nicklinson suffered a devastating stroke in 2005. He wanted to end his life but could not do so without help. The High Court refused to state that it would be lawful for a doctor to help him end his life, so he took matters into his own hands and died by voluntarily stopping eating and drinking. In 2014, two years after his death, the Supreme Court made clear that a doctor may not advise a patient how to kill themselves but could 'give objective advice about the clinical options (such as sedation and other palliative care), which would be available if a patient were to reach a settled decision to kill himself' and that 'a person who is legally and mentally competent is entitled to refuse food and water and to reject any … treatment, including artificial feeding, even though without it he will die.'[6] Current guidance from the British Medical Association (BMA) published in 2019 states that:

> an informed refusal [of care or treatment] by a competent adult must be respected, even if it will result in serious injury or death. This includes a competent refusal of foods and fluids. In these cases, it would be appropriate to discuss with the patient in advance what pain and symptom relief will be available at such a point in time that it becomes necessary.

In terms of offering sedation to patients, the BMA's advice to doctors also states:

---

[6] R (on the application of Nicklinson and another) (Appellants) v. Ministry of Justice (Respondent), 25 June 2014, www.supremecourt.uk/cases/docs/uksc-2013-0235-judgment.pdf, p. 99

continuous or palliative sedation may be offered to patients who are very close to death and experience distressing symptoms which cannot be effectively controlled by other measures. This is a serious decision which requires careful examination of doctors' motives and the availability of possible alternatives.

It would be inappropriate, for example, to provide sedation, or to offer to or agree to provide sedation before such a point in time that it becomes necessary. To do so may in some circumstances, e.g. when combined with a refusal of food and fluids, be construed as indistinguishable from assisted suicide. This would not prevent a doctor from agreeing in advance to palliate pain and discomfort, should the need for symptom management arise.[7]

I can see that it is a fine line. So everything comes down to your own personal medical caregiver, and usually that would be your GP, but organisations like Compassion in Dying can help people explore the care and support they will need to have in place should someone wish to stop eating and drinking. For example, Sarah Malik suggests that it is key to have these final par discussions in advance with your family, your GP and, where appropriate,

[7] 'Responding to patient requests for assisted dying: guidance for doctors', BMA, updated 2019, www.bma.org.uk/media/1424/bma-guidance-on-responding-to-patient-requests-for-assisted-dying-for-doctors.pdf

a hospice or palliative care team too. This goes back to earlier sections of this book, where I discussed the importance of consistency of care because doctors also need to see consistency in their patient's thoughts. In my opinion, no GP should be afraid of patients wanting some control at the end of life, no matter how awkward or emotional the conversation, and should support them, within reason and the law, in their decision-making over their own bodies and how they wish to live, or indeed die.

Sarah Malik clarified so much for me by talking through VSED. She made me realise that there are options for those of us who have reached the end of our line in terms of adapting. The preparation that she talked about, like speaking to your GP, resonated for me, because if I chose something like VSED, that's what I would be doing anyway – preparing my daughters, talking with my doctor, making sure my wishes were known and clear. It was also comforting to hear from her that, for some people, VSED is just the natural way to die rather than an alternative to assisted dying.

Just by having that choice – not even taking it – I felt suddenly so much more empowered than I did at the beginning of writing this book because of the knowledge I've gained.

Discovering that in the eyes of the law, capacity is fluid was also a comfort to me. So many healthcare managers and care-home managers say that the people in their care have no capacity, and that's not true, but I was beginning to doubt my own understanding of it. I've always said it's fluid, and Sarah put it in a nutshell when she said the Mental Capacity Act states capacity is judged decision by decision.

Just to be able to have these conversations with people like Sarah or Catherine Forest releases me from the grasp of dementia. This is why these conversations are so important, because if you're able to talk about it, the medical profession and the law as it stands no longer has that hold over you.

It was also interesting what Sarah told me about terminal agitation, and how some medical staff may not treat VSED in the same way that they treat ordinary deaths, where they would let relatives know that this is a natural stage of dying, just as there are natural stages of birth. But without the clinical guidance that medics so desperately need, they cannot support a relative watching someone die after choosing to stop eating and drinking by saying: 'Please don't worry about this agitation, it's absolutely normal and we'll sedate him to make him more comfortable.' These things are hard to talk about, but if we don't talk about them, how do we know that terminal agitation can be a very natural part of dying?

If I had reached the end of this book and I was booking a ticket to Switzerland, it would mean that I had heard nothing that had given me hope, but instead each conversation I had consolidated what I know is right, and made me more confident that I know what I want for myself.

I may have to choose VSED in the future as the only option open to me if society and the government fail to see the release and kindness that assisted dying would allow people, or I may not.

But that is a conversation for the future.

# 5

# CONVERSATIONS ON LIFE

We were perhaps halfway through the writing of this book when I received a message that I had always dreaded. I knew, in that intuitive way only a good friend does, when I saw my friend Julie's name come up on my phone one evening that the news wasn't good. And sadly, I was right. Her son Jason, forty-seven, had died. He had been in hospital more times than I could remember, his mum always fighting on his behalf for his right to live. Finally, his body had given up.

In that moment in my armchair, as the tears poured down my cheeks listening to Julie's own heartbroken voice on my phone, I was sent spinning back decades to a sunny day in a house my family had just moved into. We had been (almost) a family of four then, unaware that that would shrink to three within three short years, that I would be left alone in that house with my two girls. For now, we went from room to room excitedly, Sarah not more than three years old, Gemma still to be born. This three-bedroom detached house in Newport Pagnell seemed enormous compared to the little two-bedroom bungalow we had packed up and left. From my new bedroom window, I clutched my bump and looked out at the back garden, messy and overgrown with weeds — I would soon sort that out.

My own garden was put to shame by the garden next door: neat and tidy, all straight lines, a picture-perfect lawn, so unlike our own. A pretty, petite woman with perfectly highlighted hair was out in the garden. I had seen her before with a toddler. He was around the same age as Sarah, but this time she was bending down to help her older son onto his tricycle. The boy must have been about eight. It was unusual to see a child that big requiring help — perhaps that was what had caught my eye, and I stood at the window and watched them together. She put him onto the seat and started pushing him around the garden on it. He didn't make many movements, this passenger, but the big, wide smile was matched only by his mum's as the tricycle made its slow grind up and down the garden path. There was something even then, from behind the glass of that bedroom window, that struck me as different about him. I looked back at his mother, zoomed in on the features of her face, a shadow of anxiety I hadn't noticed when I'd seen her with her toddler. Every so often the boy's younger brother toddled over to give his elder sibling a hug or a kiss. It was a sweet

scene, and my concentration was broken only by Sarah
unpacking her toys in her new bedroom.

The woman's name was Julie, and we got to know
each over the garden fence as we pegged out washing
or watched our children play on sunny afternoons. Her
boys were Jason and Ryan. Jason, I would later learn,
was their miracle child. Born with a rare condition, he
wasn't supposed to survive his baby years. As he grew
older, he could only shuffle around, he couldn't speak or
hear, and he would never walk. As the years went by, he
was more and more reliant on his parents, and yet the joy
he found in life was unquestionable. We enjoyed many
'conversations' simply by him giving us a thumbs-up.

As the months and then summers and then the years
went by, as Julie and her husband, Terry, had another son,
Alec, and I was left alone in that house as a single mum,
Jason still thrived. His parents and his siblings learned
the importance of living in each day, of valuing that present moment, that time with Jason, and still he exceeded
anyone's expectations. Yes, there were challenges, hospital visits, operations; his parents had to carry him to
the toilet and back; his needs became more complex and
as he grew bigger and taller, those demands on his poor
mum's back became weightier. But she never flinched
and neither did Terry. They were just so grateful to still
have their boy.

Julie and Terry welcomed us into their extended family, and in return I learned the ropes – like how to let the air out of Jason's stoma bag so it didn't burst. That way his parents could enjoy a much-needed night off while I babysat for them. Terry taught me DIY, and Julie's brother, Robin, taught me how to take care of my car.

In the end we took a fence panel down between our gardens, just so the kids could run between our two homes. In many ways we were one big, happy family. We'd drop the kids off at school together in the morning as we put the world to rights, and even supermarket-shopped together, Terry picking us both up in the car, laden down with carrier bags, and dividing whose was whose once we got home and opened the boot.

Jason's condition never improved – it would only ever get worse – yet he still relished life: the most simple of things, especially Jelly Tots and the jigsaws he loved to do, the concentration on his face as he went row by row, picking up the pieces so carefully between finger and thumb and putting them into place until the picture was complete. Jason defied the medics. How many times had his parents been told to expect the worst? And yet he always came home.

By the time he was in his twenties, the lifting and carrying became too much. Julie and Terry fought the council for permission to build an extension so Jason could sleep downstairs and have his own bathroom. Julie would be up every hour to see to him in the night, but on one night she didn't hear that he was in trouble. She woke suddenly, got to the top of the stairs and there, as clear as day, was a ghostly figure at the foot of the stairs, beckoning her down, and disappearing as she approached. She found Jason in his room, in desperate need of help. I've always found that story incredible. Perhaps that was Jason's guardian angel.

While Sarah, Gemma, Ryan and Alec grew up and left home and passed all those milestones we witness as parents, Jason stayed at home with his mum and dad; their devotion to their son, their willingness to spend a life living day by day, meant he had survived decades longer than he might have done otherwise.

The pain in Julie's voice was so apparent when she broke the news to me of his death, and I would have done anything in that moment to have collapsed those years between us – and the miles now – and to have been able to hop across our gardens to give her a hug.

The fact that Jason died during the writing of this book reminded me of two things. The first being the importance of choice. I have spoken throughout this book of what life means to me now, what my own personal dealbreakers are, how I choose to live my remaining time. For some people, a life like Jason's would be their personal dealbreaker, but Jason didn't have that choice — he was trapped in a body that failed him from the start. Julie and Terry were his voice for nearly five decades, but he found joy in the smallest of moments. We are all capable of that to a certain extent, and that's one thing that we forget when we are bogged down by the minutiae of life. What a reminder he was to all of us. And that's the second thing: the importance of living in the now. Dementia has taught me that. I have said from the start that I could not predict the future once I had been diagnosed. I had no crystal ball, and the nature of the disease meant I had no choice but to live in the moment — a bit like Jason. Perhaps he has been my inspiration all these years.

As much as I believe I should have the right to choose death over life, people have the right to choose life over death. Julie and Terry chose life for Jason — again and again — and what a life they gave him.

It was Wednesday evening as I sat in front of the telly, willing that blue splodge that looked as if a great bottle of ink had been tipped across North-East England to disappear from the weather map.

*They'll never let me do it now*, I thought to myself, feeling despondent about the rain that was forecast for Sunday.

I opened my iPad and typed in the website of the wing-walk company, anticipating having to rebook my much-awaited flight. I often feel that now — a sense of impatience, a desire to hurry these experiences. There is no time to waste.

*Unless*, I thought, *they could do it* before *the weekend?*

I sent an email and within minutes I had a response. We were on for 1 p.m. Friday.

*Perfect*, I thought.

The following day, Gemma came over to dye my hair pink for the occasion. I was a little sceptical about shocking-pink hair, so instead I instructed her only to add a few drops, but later, as I walked around the village, catching my reflection in the windows, I chastised myself: *Should have been braver.*

On Friday morning when I woke up at 4.25 a.m., time on my hands because I'd woken so early, the dawn sky matching my new hair, I resolved to be braver. After all, I was going 600 feet up in the air strapped to the wing of an aeroplane that day. I doubled the number of drops and dyed my hair again. Still not shocking pink, but a much deeper, richer colour.

*They will be sure to spot me up in the air now*, I told myself.

Sarah arrived later that morning to drive me to the airfield in Lincolnshire. We set off in the car, chatting away, only for me to realise that I'd forgotten two vital things – first, the letter from my GP stating that I was fit to fly, and second, my friend Elaine's photo. I had met Elaine at the Minds and Voices, the support group in York for people living with dementia. Elaine had always saluted my sense of adventure, my willingness to take risks; simply because I no longer had anything to lose, the fear had evaporated, and so when she died recently, I had promised her husband, Eric, I would take her up in the plane in my pocket.

Sarah and I did an about-turn, racing back to the house, which meant – coupled with the traffic on the Humber Bridge – I finally arrived at the airfield frazzled and stressed with minutes to spare.

We made our way to the front desk, where staff asked for my GP form before anything else (thank goodness we'd gone back for it).

'Sorry we're late,' I said, dreading the moment they might say I'd missed my turn.

'Don't worry – just relax,' the lady behind the desk said, 'and have a look at some of our safety videos.'

I sat down next to a man probably three decades younger than me. He wore a big fleecy jumper and an anxious smile. He was also about to take to the skies, and as we watched the videos we joked together about how on earth we would remember all that we needed to – of course, he had no idea it would be a lot harder for me than him. Apparently there were five vital things that I needed to remember. Five – that sounded impossible. So instead I picked two – hoping they were the right two to pick – 'don't touch the safety pin on the straps or it will undo your fastenings' and 'arms out, thumbs down, if you've had enough or you're in trouble'. They sounded like important things to remember.

After watching the videos, Sarah and I went outside and sat on a bench with some of the other people who were about to do their own flights. One lady sat in a brightly coloured jester's hat and introduced herself as Helen. It was her friend, Liz, who was doing the flight, but Helen was so nervous for her, she felt nauseous. When I told her I was about to go up too, she looked even more petrified.

It turned out that Liz was doing her wing walk as a wacky idea to celebrate her fiftieth birthday and, even more excitingly, she was raising money for Dementia UK. The second I told her that I had dementia, she was overwhelmed with emotion, and from that moment on we were firm friends, bouncing off each other's enthusiasm and getting even more excited for our own flights.

When Liz's name was called, I listened carefully to everything the instructors told her, and watched how she was shown to climb onto the plane, as everything I had learned in the safety video had long left my head, except those two things: don't touch the safety pins; arms out, thumbs down if you're in trouble. As Liz's yellow plane started rumbling along, her smile seemed as wide as the runway.

Moments later, my silver plane rolled up beside us.

'I think I'll get you another fleece,' one of the instructors said. 'You can never be too warm up there in the sky.'

I looked up to see Liz's plane climbing up towards the clouds.

The instructor helped me onto the plane, strapped me onto the wing, handed me ear plugs, adjusted my goggles, and then I felt the rumble of the plane's engine beneath my feet. No going back now.

'Can you remember how you show the pilot that you want to come down?' he asked, though he looked doubtful.

Thank goodness he'd asked me for one of the two things I'd remembered. I immediately put out both arms with my thumbs down. He looked relieved and clambered down from the wings of the plane.

Finally, it was time for us to taxi down the runway, a bumpy trip along the grass which jolted me this way and that, but I managed a final wave to Sarah and Liz's friend, Helen – who looked far more nervous than I felt. The wheels of the biplane picked up speed, the wind rushed past my ears, the vibration of the engine at my feet travelled through my whole body, and then suddenly, we had lift off. Up, up, up we went, banking slightly to the right to give me a view of the runway we had just left. We climbed higher, higher still, a green carpet created from the tops of trees spread out before me.

Still we ascended in the air; silence from the ground, the strength of the wind pinning my body to the wings of the plane. I knew I was meant to keep my arms out straight, but the sheer power blowing against me made that impossible and so I satisfied myself to keep my elbows tucked in at my waist, my lower arms sticking out. That would have to do.

And still we climbed higher, the force of the wind whipped at my face, taking my huge smile up and down and side to side, and as the plane banked left and right I saw tiny dots of people watching and waving from the ground. But the smile remained there, pinned to my face by the wind, up in the air, the clouds within touching distance, my mind empty of thoughts except the sheer brilliance of this one, amazing moment – and how adept I have become at living in these moments.

Before I knew it, the plane started its descent, down and down and down it went, until the grass beneath us met the wheels of the plane and – *bump, bump* – we landed. I waved towards Sarah to let her know I'd survived as we taxied over to meet the staff.

The instructors had to help me off the plane because my legs had forgotten how to stay upright all on their own, but when Sarah greeted me with my walking stick, I could barely find the words to express what a magical experience it had been.

'Wow,' I kept saying, over and over.

The pilot came over with a video he'd made of the flight, and later on, when I watched it at home, I could hear him saying: 'Just awesome.'

And it really was. I have said before that dementia has taken fear away from me in so many areas: fear of the dark, fear of animals, fear of death. It means I can do these wacky things because the disease has pushed all the 'what ifs' out of my head and, yes, replaced them with something that feels like wads of cotton wool some days, but we find the positives where we can. If dementia has also made me more daring, if it has helped me to walk across hot coals, jump out of an aeroplane to skydive or stand on the wings of a plane as it soars 600 feet high in the sky, then I will see that for what it is – a gift.

When it is time to release that hard grasp on life, when it is time to open your fingers a little, to feel more insistently the sands of time running through them, then there is no fear, because you feel more deeply that what will be will be, for all of us; you know more intuitively that control is – and always was – nothing more than an illusion. And it is then that you really get on with the business of living.

# ONE LAST THING... EPILOGUE

The world was yet to wake as I left my front door that morning. The trees were black, silhouetted against a deep inky-blue sky. It is not unusual for me to leave my house while others are still blanketed in unbroken sleep – *I remember that.*

Crossing the threshold of my front door represents a break from my constant companion these days. I leave dementia at home as I turn the key in the lock, leave it padding around the carpet, pottering from room to room. When my first footstep hits the cold morning pavement, when I feel the still of the air on my cheeks, it is an escape, it is autonomy. *I am still self-sufficient.*

Throughout the summer, I had heard fewer birds than normal, the dawn chorus more dim than the usual din, as if nature had turned down the volume. I had told myself that the drought had forced them to migrate to some-where with more rainfall, in that way that nature adapts to climate – in that way we all do, often unwittingly – yet that morning in particular, the trees were filled with their welcome chatter and as I set off down the lane, I smiled to hear them once again keeping me company.

I decided to go to the far end of the village first. I trundled by the playing fields, along the narrow track to the open field at the bottom. It was still too early for sunrise, but the indigo sky was lightening and the clouds were gathering lilac frills; *there was light somewhere breaking through.*

I headed along the back lane and turned into the gallops, where a heavy low mist hovered over the field. The horses were just waking and looking for breakfast, and somewhere on the horizon the sun was slowly keeping its promise to break into the day, *just like it does every day.*

I stood at the edge of that autumn field, my cheeks cold with the first breaths of winter, the camera in my hand clicking to capture all the colours that bleached the morning as the sun started to rise where the hills met the skyline. I waited for that moment, for the first golden threads of a new day to pierce those clouds, and then there it was in all its fiery brilliance. *A new day — a gift.*

I felt a burning desire then, a need to revisit an old haunt, to walk another path I was once so familiar with, to feel the track under the soles of my feet, *to see if I could still remember.*

I caught the early bus to York that morning as the world woke up, as people new from sleep mounted the bus, still fuzzy from dreams. I watched them as they took their seats around me, they stared out of the window, or mostly at their phones, the world rushing by, on automatic, as nature on the other side of the glass tried her best to seduce them with her beauty. It's often easy to miss.

*I know I used to.*

I disembarked the bus in the centre of York and let my feet lead the way, hoping that I could still flex that muscle memory – was it there, imprinted within me?

There were more people in York: they hurried to get to work, heads down, bustling past, unlike me with my walking stick. I wanted to turn then, to go home, back to safety, but the thought of that silent companion that awaited me behind the door was enough to convince me to keep to the path.

I headed towards the river, past pubs that seemed so familiar – I saw a woman sitting at one of the outdoor tables with friends, yet when I looked back again, she was gone. I went further into the city, following tree-lined paths, one split into two – for pedestrians, one for cyclists – and then I saw her again, just a split second as she rushed past on her pink bicycle. *I knew her.*

I was beside the water now. We walked together, me carried along by its flow. It was too complicated these days to go against its current; better to drift with it, see where it took me, past the moored boats – I remember them – and then yes, I remember that blue bridge.

I stopped and stared, let the river carry on without me for a few moments. There is nothing particularly beautiful about the design and structure of that bridge, yet it greeted me *like an old friend*.

I caught up with the river, one foot in front of another, then through the trees I caught sight of it – the Milennium Bridge. I soon reached it, and when I did, my feet on that old familiar tarmac, it was another day, a sunny one, and the sky was filled with the sound of chatter of people, not birds, of children watching the swans drift by with delight, and parents handing the last of old bread crusts to throw to them. I had a flask in my hand and was joining the crowds to sit and watch the world go by, *just as I always had*.

There is a wooden plinth that runs the length of the bridge, and so I sat down there, *and that's when I saw her again*. This time she was running, a smile on her face, the wind in her hair – she looked so carefree, so happy. *I knew her instantly.*

'Morning,' she said as she passed.

And I smiled at her as she went and wondered if I should tell her that it will be just over this bridge in a few moments that she will first fall, that she won't know why, that she will stumble to the doctors' surgery, all bloody and bruised, and the nurse who patches her up will joke about accidents out running, that they will both laugh it off, that'll she'll think it's a one-off. But in the back of her mind, she will already know.

No, perhaps it's better to let her run on, unhindered by the future.

And yet, there are other things I could say... *that it won't be that brain tumour that you first fear. That I understand why, at fifty-six, that is your first thought – why else would your brain stop talking to your legs? That it will be another eighteen months from now that they finally tell you, when you sit alone in a room with a consultant who explains what this disease is that has invaded your brain, that it was nothing you have done, or haven't done; that you were simply unlucky.*

*Unlucky. You'll tell yourself that word too. But I want to tell you a story with a different ending to the one you've already written in your head. I want to tell you that although you've never heard of young-onset dementia, they will soon be three words that slip so easily from your tongue. I want to tell you that what will at first feel like a curse will in many ways bring you joys you simply couldn't imagine – yes, joys.*

*I know you'll need time to come to terms with your diagnosis, I know for a long time you will think it's the end – it will be so typical of you to get all your paperwork together – but will you believe me if I say that it will just be the beginning? A new beginning. Yes, it won't be without its challenges, and there will be lows – there's no getting away from that – but there will be highs too. Quite literally, though – I'll come to that.*

*First your two girls – the two most important people in your life – the first thing your mind will rush to is the day you no longer know them. But let me tell you: you always will – love* is a bond that even a cruel disease like dementia cannot break. I know the thought of forgetting their birthdays is impossible to you now, but it will be okay, you will find a way – you know how that has always been your mantra? Well, now will be the time to employ it more than ever. You will set an alarm on your iPad to make sure you don't forget; you will make yourself useful to them in inventive ways you could never imagine; there will be so many happy times ahead, and they will make you more proud that you can ever know right now.

I know how you tell yourself now that the only person you can ever trust completely is yourself – I know people have hurt and disappointed you in your life, which has made you come to this conclusion – but I'm asking you to trust me now.

You've always been so private, not aloof, just happier in your own company, but let me tell you of this new person you will become. It will be one of the first things the girls notice about you: how outgoing you suddenly are, how willing you will be to share your story – but that will be out of necessity, because you will be so stunned by the lack of awareness about the disease, not just from members of the public, but unfortunately more from the medical profession itself.

You will be an educator, a campaigner, an inspiration to many, many people who will be just down the road from you in their own diagnoses. Yes, you will sink into a deep depression when you are first diagnosed when the doctors tell you there is no hope, but once you pull yourself out of it, you will light the way for others. You will prevent them suffering depression, you *will receive an email from a lady who will tell you that where she once feared her own diagnosis, she now says:* Bring it on, *and that, and so many other emails you will receive from people, will make it all worthwhile.*

*I know you can't imagine all this, not right now, but trust me.*

*You know how you've always liked to be organised? Well, that will now pay dividends. There will be countless times when you will evade this uninvited guest in your brain, simply through tricks that you will employ to help you organise your days, travel, and, most importantly, live alone, because I know – I know – how much you value your independence. When you forget how to tie your shoelaces, Sarah will find you elastic ones. When you walk through a door in your new house and forget where it leads to or where you've just come from, you'll get a screwdriver and take the damn door off. No problem will be insurmountable to you – in fact, you'll revel in the challenges dementia brings.*

*You only have a handful of close friends now, but this new disease will introduce you to so many more dear people that you will love as if you have known them your whole life. Innovations in Dementia – remember that name: you will meet wonderful, dedicated people there who you can trust.*

*I know there are times now when you switch off your light at night and the room is flooded with darkness that makes you ache with loneliness, but what if I told you that you would never feel lonely again, that the community you are about to meet will keep you company throughout this disease, that in those sleepless nights you will only have to open your phone and find a friend* on social media. Yes, social media; long gone will be that techno-phobe you — you will embrace technology: your smartphone, your iPad, your camera. You will start writing a blog just a few weeks after your diagnosis that will be read throughout the world.

I know now, as you run over this bridge, you'll be like everyone else, wishing your working week away, living for the weekend, and it pains me to have to tell you that you won't be able to con-tinue working. The world will not have yet caught up with how useful people with dementia can still be; that they don't lose all their skills overnight simply because they've been diagnosed with a disease in their brain; that just like we have to adapt, workplaces will need to learn to do that too; but you will help people to learn that. You will help employers to support their staff; you will help train nurses to look after their patients; you will advise hospitals and care homes on designs for people with dementia; you will offer up your brain for academics to poke and prod (okay, that bit might happen after you have died!), and you will be rewarded for all this work with two honorary doctorates from two universities, which will make you want to burst with pride.

There will be bad days, I can't lie to you, and as the disease progresses, they will become more common. In a few months' time you will step out of your office one day and not recognise any of your surroundings. You will stumble along the corridor to the loos, hoping no one stops you on the way to chat, because you have no idea who anyone is, and you will lock yourself inside a cubicle and wait for that fog to lift, for the world to come back into focus – and it will.

But there will be a day when it won't, and it may be many, many years down the line, and even I don't know when, and that will be the only thing left that scares you. You will plead with people to understand that, and they will tell you that you will be happy even when that happens, even when you go over the edge, but they don't know you like I do – they don't know that even if I stopped you now on this bridge and asked for your thoughts on assisted dying, you'd give me the same answer: that people should have choice, that people shouldn't be made to suffer. The world still has a lot of catching up to do. You'll hope the last book you write will help people to realise that.

Just hold onto the fact that, for now, those fogs will lift. Likewise, try not to mourn for too long the things you will need to let go of – other things will come and replace them. I can almost smell that lemon drizzle cake you've left cooling on the worktop at home, and though you won't be able to follow recipes any more, or decorate your own house, or drive your beloved car, I hope you will see that these other gains I talk about will go some way to making up for all the losses.

You'll replace driving with walking, and you'll walk for miles each day. You'll still travel to your beloved paradise – the Lake District – though not with your best friend, Sylvia, and I can't explain why now, because some things in the future are better left untold. Wait for that story to unfold and be brave – for both of you: some of life's twists and turns are better met in the moment, but you will cope, just like you always have.

You'll find a wonderful little B & B in Keswick called Appletrees and there you will be looked after; they'll even put a pillowcase over the TV in the corner, so the black screen doesn't look like a big hole in the wall to you, because that's the other thing I need to tell you about dementia – it's not just memory. It changes the way you walk (which is why you're about to fall for the first time), the way you hear, what you see (you'll adopt a thirty-minute rule to see if things you're seeing are really there, or are just hallucinations) and even how you taste. And that's one thing I do need to break to you: your beloved Yorkshire Tea will be lost to you, and even in spite of all the other losses, I know you'll find this one of the hardest to let go of. You'll try all sorts of other teas, but nothing will replace that 'hug-in-a-mug'. But you will be content eventually just to sit with a weak brew between your hands, simply for the comfort and companionship of it.

Dementia will bring you so many adventures. You know how you enjoyed the Three Peaks Challenge? Well, what if I said that would be nothing compared to some of the other things you will do. If I said to you now that you'd jump out of a plane and parachute back down to earth, I know you would be horrified, but there we are, life holds surprises, both bad and good (did I mention that you will meet a Hollywood superstar and she'll mention you in her BAFTA award acceptance speech? Perhaps I'll save that story – don't want you getting ahead of yourself).

*You've crossed the bridge now, and I can only see the back of you as you disappear almost out of sight. Sometimes I feel sad that I've lost you, that I resemble you so little, but then the glass-half-full person is a trait we still share and that's a comfort, and our love for our daughters: that's one thing we will always have in common; that is something this disease will never take from us. You won't be scared of anything any more, because the worst thing that could possibly happen to you is dementia and that's already happened. But when you read the words that I have written here... are you sure it was the worst thing that could happen to you?*

Am I sure?

*You're about to take that last step off the bridge now, and before you go, I must tell you one last thing. You will meet a writer called Anna Wharton and she will tell you that you have a book in you, but even she won't know then that it will actually be three, and that two of them will be* Sunday Times *bestsellers, and all that wisdom you have accumulated from this life-changing event you will commit to those pages with her help, and that will be your legacy. That is what you'll leave behind, and while you're still alive, it will be life-changing.*

*There, you've just fallen, I can see you on the ground now. I wish I could get up and help, but look, you're already doing it yourself, stumbling a bit, but you're up on your feet, you're brushing yourself off, you are turning to look at the pavement, wondering where you slipped. But I can tell you there is nothing there: it is this disease inside your brain that made you do it.*

*You haven't got long to wait to find that out, but when you do, promise me you'll remember everything I have told you...*

I got up from my seat with my walking stick, I checked my watch and saw there was a bus in thirty minutes. I decided to go back the way I had come. For a moment, I turned to see that woman, but there was nothing there, nobody at all – yet I said goodbye to her anyway, that *somebody I used to know.*

# RESOURCES

The following information provides an overview for key elements of Advance Care Planning. There is information on general principles, support for Advance Care Planning Conversations as well as more specific Advance Care Planning resources, such as making an Advance Decision to Refuse Treatment. There are many more resources available nationally and internationally and your local GP or Hospice may have information relevant to your local area.

Advance Care Planning is a process, not a form, and will change as life evolves. It's part of planning throughout life, not something only for those at the end of life. To take the first steps, start talking about what matters most to you with the people you love.


## GENERAL ADVANCE CARE PLANNING

NHS information about an Advance Statement of Wishes and Preferences: www.nhs.uk/conditions/end-of-life-care/advance-statement

A podcast discussing how Joy Lists can help create an Advance Statement of Wishes and Preferences: speakforme.co.uk/podcast-episode-21

Templates and information about Advance Care Planning: advancecareplan.org.uk/advance-care-plan-journey

NHS information on Universal Principles for Advance Care Planning: www.england.nhs.uk/wp-content/

uploads/2022/03/universal-principles-for-advance-care-planning.pdf

Palliative Care for People with Learning Disabilities includes information on Advance Care Planning: www.pcpld.org/links-and-resources

Conversations About Advance Care Planning with Clare Fuller, a podcast exploring what Advance Care Planning is, how to do it and why it matters: speakforme.co.uk/podcast-2

Hospice UK's Dying Matters campaign is working with you to create an open culture in which we're comfortable talking about death, dying and grief: www.hospiceuk.org/our-campaigns/dying-matters

## ADVANCE DECISION TO REFUSE TREATMENT

NHS information about Advance Decision to Refuse Treatment: www.nhs.uk/conditions/end-of-life-care/advance-decision-to-refuse-treatment

Compassion in Dying: compassionindying.org.uk/how-we-can-help/living-will-advance-decision

A podcast exploring Advance Decision to Refuse Treatment: speakforme.co.uk/podcast-episode-7

## ORGAN DONATION

NHS information about Organ Donation: www.organdonation.nhs.uk

Information about the law and Organ Donation: www.organdonation.nhs.uk/uk-laws/organ-donation-law-in-england

A podcast exploring hope and transition after unexpected death: speakforme.co.uk/podcast-episode-20

## DO NOT ATTEMPT CARDIOPULMONARY RESUSCITATION (DNACPR)

Resuscitation Council UK information on DNACPR and ReSPECT: www.resus.org.uk/public-resource/cpr-decisions-and-dnacpr

NHS information on Do Not Attempt Cardiopulmonary Resuscitation: www.nhs.uk/conditions/do-not-attempt-cardiopulmonary-resuscitation-dnacpr-decisions/

Podcast with Dr Zoe Fritz exploring the development of ReSPECT: speakforme.co.uk/podcast-episode-39

## LEGACY MAKING

A podcast exploring memory-making: speakforme.co.uk/podcast-episode-18

Digital Legacy: digitallegacyassociation.org

## LASTING POWER OF ATTORNEY

Information on how to make, register or end a lasting power of attorney: www.gov.uk/power-of-attorney

Speak For Me LPA: speakforme.co.uk/services

Lasting Power of Attorney campaign: powerofattorney.campaign.gov.uk

## SUPPORTING ADVANCE CARE PLANNING CONVERSATIONS

Marie Curie Talk About cards: www.mariecurie.org. uk/talkabout

Dying Matters Planning Ahead tool: advancecare planning.org.uk/planning-ahead

What Matters Conversations: www.whatmatters conversations.org

What Matters to You: www.whatmatterstoyou.scot

*Listen*, Kathryn Mannix (HarperCollins, 2022)

## SUPPORTING MAKING AN ADVANCE CARE PLAN

My Care Matters Handbook: mycarematters.org/store/ posters-prints-books/my-future-care-handbook

MyWishes: www.mywishes.co.uk

Advice and support in making an Advance Care Plan: speakforme.co.uk/advance-care-planning-service

This list of resources was kindly compiled by Advance Care Planning Advocate Clare Fuller. Clare is an End of Life Care Expert, patient rights campaigner, educator, and Lasting Power of Attorney Consultant. You can find out more about Clare and her work by visiting www.speakforme.co.uk

# ACKNOWLEDGEMENTS

No one knows what hand life will deal them. A curved ball here and there in the form of divorce or unexpected death. For me, the one single meeting that changed everything for me was sitting in that consulting room and hearing that diagnosis of dementia. I thought it was the end as no one told me any different. How wrong I was. Instead, here I am, writing acknowledgments, not for the first or second time, but for the third, and indeed, final time.

My life was enriched beyond belief when I met my partner-in-writing, Anna Wharton, all those years ago. From humble beginnings we have now become a force to be reckoned with and I hope our partnership will change people's views and understanding once again in this book. To me, Anna is now a friend for life and I can count on one hand people I've allowed to become that close.

Thank you to Robert Caskie for looking after us so well. Also to the team at Bloomsbury, none more so than Alexis Kirschbaum for believing in us a final time. Plus all the wonderful team behind Alexis, especially Jonny Coward who keeps me organised, but also Shanika

Hyslop, Kate Quarry, Francisco Vilhena, Ariel Pakier, Akua Boateng, David Mann and Stephanie Rathbone.

Huge thanks to all the amazing people who agreed to be interviewed in our writing of this book, without which we could never have written such a powerful message. They include my best friend Sylvia, for posthumously allowing me to share a little of her story, along with her husband, David. My dearest friends, Julie and Terry, for allowing me to share Jason's story. Catherine Wood, for sharing her experiences as both a carer and her PhD research. Jon Underwood posthumously for setting up UK Death Cafes and his mother Susan Barksy Reid. Aly Dickinson and End of Life Doula UK. Esther Ramsay-Jones for sharing her dear mum, Joyce's story. Sarah Drummond and her sisters for sharing their mother Heather's story. Ellie Ball and Sarah Malik from Compassion in Dying. Clare Fuller for generously giving her time to sort out my Advance Planning paperwork. Molly Bartlett, Kathryn Mannix, Rebecca Langley, Peter Hallgarten, Jane Gould, Paul Blomfield MP and Baroness Ilora Finlay of Llanduff, all for giving up their valuable time to speak to me.

My penultimate thanks must go to all my friends living with dementia. Especially my three Amigos: Dory, Gail and George. Without them, I'd be lost and lonely, alongside Innovations in Dementia who are responsible for the DEEP Network of groups for people living with dementia. The small but exquisitely formed group of people who make up Innovations in Dementia, a not-for-profit organisation, Philly, Rachael, Rachel, Steve and Damian, cannot possible realise just how much they have helped so many people living with dementia, they've given us a true voice and continually encourage and enable us to speak out and be heard – something no other charity does better.

But finally, as always, my love and thanks must go to the most important five in my life. Firstly, the most important people in my life, Sarah, Gemma and Stuart. Without their support, their understanding and their laughter, my world would be an empty shell and I would not be where I am today. And now to the animals, Billy and Merlin whose unconditional love and furry cuddles bring me so much joy.

Please feel free to read and follow my countless escapades at www.whichmeamitoday.wordpress.com

Or follow me on Twitter, my silent world of conversation @WendyPMitchell

# A NOTE ON THE AUTHOR

Wendy Mitchell spent twenty years as a non-clinical team leader in the NHS before being diagnosed with young-onset dementia in July 2014 at the age of fifty-eight. Shocked by the lack of awareness about the disease, both in the community and in hospitals, she vowed to spend her time raising awareness about dementia and encouraging others to see that there is life after a diagnosis. In 2019 she was awarded an honorary Doctor of Health by the University of Bradford for her contribution to research. She has two daughters and lives in Yorkshire.